WITH THE MAKERS OF TEXAS

TEXAS

E. C. BARKER
&
H. E. BOLTON

Copano Bay Press
2018

ISBN 978-1-941324-13-4
Design and new material copyright
2018 - Copano Bay Press

INTRODUCTION

Among the improvements in the methods of teaching history that have been so marked in recent years, there is perhaps none that has been of greater value than the introduction of the use of sources. Nothing has gone further towards making it possible to obtain from the study of the subject a maximum of that culture which properly belongs thereto. One result of the improvement has been to give the student a sense of reality in the past and of naturalness in the social processes with which he has to deal that could never be attainable through secondary narratives or descriptions. In the utterances of the contemporaries the vanished age returns, the old quarrels are fought out, and the old ideals prevail; and the earnest listener, be he man or boy, hears and understands. His sympathies are aroused, and his humanity is quickened into healthier growth.

Another result has been to train the student's judgment in a way that was not possible by the old-fashioned means of using a single text; for by this method he was precluded from the exercise in analyzing and valuing evidence which the use of sources demands.

A good text-book is essential for teaching elementary classes in history; because in this way the organization of the subject, which is the most important desideratum, can be best effected. But the work of th teacher is less than half done if he fails to go beyond the text. The student taught in such a way is liable to acquire an unquestioning, and often a genuinely timid, dependence on authority. The teaching which has an effect like this is worse than incomplete or even useless; it is positively harmful. No qualities are better worth cultivation in any one that is being trained for the duties of life than broad human sympathy and robust self-dependence in thinking.

Experts in historical pedagogy differ concerning the extent to which sources may be advantageously used, and some are not inclined to use them at all, except in advanced work. The best answer to these doubters will be found in an experimental application of the theories which they deny, provided it is made under proper conditions. If the selections from the documents are of the right kind, if they are sufficiently interesting and simple—and such matter can usually be found—there need be no fear.

6

The selections in this reader will, as I believe, stand the test. The history of Texas is marked at every stage by individual and social experiences that are just of the kind to awaken an intense interest on the part of the young, and many fascinating narratives of these experiences have been left by the men and women who went through them. The compilers of the book have chosen well from their abundant materials, and I am sure it will be found a pleasure to the pupil that uses it, as well as a valuable aid to the teacher. To the Texan boys and girls who read these extracts, Austin and Houston will no longer be seen, as they now appear to so many of the children in our schools, like figures at twilight in a distant wood, but will become the vivid personalities, each with his strength and weakness, that they were. The motives, both the sordid and the unselfish, that gave impulse to the work of Spaniard and Anglo-American; the toil and privation by which the land was won, and the pleasures experienced in the winning; the folly of the quarrel between governor and council, and the heroism in the defense of the Alamo will alike be understood. The truth will become clear, and from the history will be gathered its right lesson and its proper inspiration.

GEORGE P. GARRISON
The University of Texas,
June 30, 1904.

PURPOSE AND PLAN

With the Makers of Texas may serve either as a reader or to supplement the history text. To fit it for a reader, selection has been made of pieces with literary merit and of varied character. And yet, they possess, with-al, a unity and localization of interest which few ordinary readers can claim. As a text for the reading class it can be most profitably used, perhaps, either in the grade preceding the study of, or by the grade actually studying, Pennybacker. If it be preferred to use the book as a supplementary work in the hands of the history class, rather than as a reader, the cross-references to Pennybacker and to Garrison will facilitate the plan.

8   The compilers have gathered copiously from every period of the State's history, and those who helped to make Texas what it is are allowed to tell in their own words of the hardships and dangers, triumphs and pleasures, of the life they lived. The selections have been arranged in six groups, corresponding with the large periods in Texas History; but it has not been the object to cover every step in the State's development. In general, little attention has been given to political history, the outlines of which can be easily gotten from the State text-book. It has been the constant aim of the compilers not to over-edit the selections, but it is hoped that they have at the same time escaped the danger of insufficiently editing them.

The general editorial plan has been this:

(1) Each piece, where its setting is not clearly shown in the text, is preceded by a brief introduction. In this

are explained the circumstances leading up to the events described, their bearing on the general history of Texas, and the connection of the writer with the story that he narrates.

(2) A list of questions follows nearly every selection and brings out its principal values. Some general questions are asked, by way of suggestion, that can not be answered directly from the text; others call for a comparison of several selections indicated by references.

(3) Difficult words—chiefly proper names—are pronounced when they first occur.

(4) Foreign or unusual words are explained. Where the explanation is brief enough it has been inserted in the text in brackets, otherwise it is placed in a foot note.

(5) To train the pupil in the organization and use of materials, frequent cross-references are made in the footnotes. Wherever possible direct references for collateral reading have been made to Pennybacker's *A New History of Texas* and to Garrison's *Texas*.

(6) The marginal synopsis furnishes a rapid summary of the selections. *[NOTE: Marginal notes have been omitted from this edition.]*

(7) The illustrations have been carefully chosen, and are intended both to instruct and to entertain. For this reason questions are asked about the pictures as well as about the text.

(8) Finally, for the benefit primarily of the teacher, specific bibliographical references have been accurately given.

Much matter, of course, has been omitted in adapting the pieces to this collection, and, on account of the elementary grade of work for which the book is designed, it has been thought best not to lessen the attractiveness of the pages by indicating the omissions.

The capitalization and punctuation are in many cases those of the compilers, and in a very few instances a difficult word has been replaced by its simpler synonym; but nothing has been added, and in all essentials the language is that of the authors.

In presenting this collection of sources the compilers are indebted to Dr. George P. Garrison, Professor of History in the University of Texas, for many helpful suggestions. To Miss Lilia M. Casis, Professor of Spanish, and Miss Ethel Zivley Rather, of the School of History, in The University of Texas, they are under obligations for some of the translations from the Spanish. They have also to thank Mr. Chas. F. Lummis, of Los Angeles, California, for the use of several interesting illustrations. And they desire to acknowledge especially the usefulness of the *Quarterly* of the Texas State Historical Association, which is a veritable mine of material on Texas history.

HERBERT EUGENE BOLTON,
EUGENE C. BARKER
The University of Texas
July 5, 1904

TABLE OF CONTENTS

CONTENTS (CONTINUED)

Contents (continued)

CONTENTS (CONTINUED)

Contents (continued)

PART SIX:
The State

I hear the tread of pioneers
Of nations yet to be;
The first low wash of waves, where soon
Shall roll a human sea.

16

The rudiments of empire here
Are plastic yet and warm;
The chaos of a mighty world
Is rounding into form.

— Whittier.

PART ONE

The Spanish and The French

A Shipwrecked Spaniard in Texas
by Alvar Nuñez Cabeza de Vaca, 1528-1534

Part One

In 1528 a Spaniard named Narvaez came to America with a large party of men to conquer and govern all the country from Florida to Mexico. After wandering about in Florida for a time, they decided to go to Mexico by sea. During the voyage most of the party were lost, but Cabeza de Vaca, one of the officers, and a few others were cast ashore on the Texas coast at an island which they named Malhado. After his return to Spain Cabeza described his experiences in a letter to the emperor, Charles V. The story given here is a part of that letter. It begins with the building of the boats at the Bay of Horses, on the Florida coast.

The governor called his men together and asked each one's opinion as to what should be done to get out of this miserable country. We agreed upon a great plan, but one that was extremely difficult to put into operation. It was to build vessels in which we might get away. Now, to all of us, this appeared almost impossible, for we did not know how to build boats, and there were no tools, nor iron, nor forge, nor tow, nor resin, nor rigging; and, above all, there was nothing to eat while building.

The next day God willed it that one of the company should come saying that he could make some pipes out of wood and rig them with deerskins, to serve as bellows. We told him to set to work and that the rest of us would make nails, saws, axes, and other tools from the stirrups, spurs, crossbows, and such other iron things as we had. For food we decided that every third day a horse should be killed and divided among those working on the boats.

We commenced the boats on the fourth of August, 1528, and worked with such diligence that, on the 20th of September, five were finished, each thirty-three feet long. We caulked them with palm fibre and pitched them with a kind of resin made from pine trees by a Greek named Don Theodoro. From the husk of the palm and from the tails and manes of the horses we made ropes and riggings; from our shirts we made sails; and from the cedars growing there, oars. We flayed the horses, taking the skins from their legs whole, and tanning them to make bottles in which to carry water. By the 22d of the month all but one horse had been consumed, and on that day we embarked. We continued in company, eating a daily allowance of half a handful of raw maize, until we lost sight of each other in a storm. The weather was so bad that it was only God's favor that kept us from all going down.

Near the dawn of day on November 6th it seemed to me that I heard the breaking of the surf. Surprised at this, I called to the master, who answered me that he believed we were near the land. We sounded and found ourselves in seven fathoms. He advised that we should keep to sea until sunrise; so I took an oar and pulled on the land side until we were a league distant. Coming near the shore again, a wave took us and threw the boat out of the water. From the violence with which she struck, nearly all

19

the people in her, who were almost dead, were roused to consciousness. Finding themselves near the shore, they began to crawl on hands and feet to the land.

There we made a fire, parched some of the maize we had brought, and found rain-water. From the warmth of the fire the people recovered their senses and began to exert themselves a little. The day on which we arrived was the 6th of November.

After the people had eaten, I ordered Oviedo, who had more strength than any of the rest, to go to some of the trees near by, climb into one of them and look about to try to gain some knowledge of the country. He did as I ordered and found that we were on an island. He saw that the land was pawed up as ground usually is where cattle range. For this reason he thought the country must be inhabited by Christians.

As we were in the condition I have described, entirely without provisions or the means of carrying any, the greater number of us naked, and the weather too severe for travel, we yielded to necessity and decided to pass the winter where we were. We also agreed that four of the strongest among us should go on to Panuco, which we thought must be near.

Part Two

I was obliged to remain with the people of this island more than a year. But, because of the hard work they put upon me and of the harsh treatment that I received, the life I led became unbearable. Besides much other labor, I had to dig up roots from below the water, and from among the cane where they grew in the ground. From this work my fingers became so worn that if only a straw touched them they would bleed. As many of the canes are broken, and as I had to go in the midst of them nearly naked, they often tore my flesh.

I therefore resolved to flee to the people of Charruco, who live in the woods on the mainland, and set to contriving a way to get over to them. When at last I reached these people affairs turned somewhat more in my favor. I began trading, and strove to make my employment profitable. Through it I not only secured food, but also received good treatment. The Indians would beg me to go from one place to another for things they needed, for, on account of continual wars, they can not go about the country nor trade much. With my goods I went into the interior as far as I pleased, and traveled along the coast forty or fifty leagues.

My principal wares were cones, pieces of sea-snail, conch shells used for knives, and fruit like a bean, which they value very highly. They use it as a medicine and in their dances and festivities. Such were the things I carried into the country. In return I got skins, ochre, with which they color their faces, sinews, cement, hard canes, of which they make arrows, flint for the arrow heads, and tassels of deer's hair.

This occupation suited me well. It gave me liberty to go where I wished, I was not obliged to work, and was no longer a slave. Wherever I went I received fair treatment, and the Indians gave me food in order to get my goods.

My main object in going about in this business was to find out how to get away. The hardships that I endured while engaged in it, as well of peril and privation as of storms and cold, it would take long to tell. Oftentimes misfortunes overtook me when alone and in the wilderness. But by the great mercy of God I came forth from them all. I was in this country nearly six years, alone among the Indians and naked like them.

Discussion

1. Describe the building of the boats at the Bay of Horses.
2. How long did it take to build them?
3. How long was it from the embarkation of the men to the time when they were cast ashore?
4. What do you suppose the animals were that pawed up the land on the island?
5. Describe the hardships endured by Cabeza while he was a slave.
6. What were his wares while a peddler?
7. Who wrote this story? When?

Indian Life in Texas
by Alvar Nuñez Cabeza de Vaca, 1528

PART ONE

Cabeza de Vaca here tells of some of the strange things he saw while he lived among the Texas Indians.

To this island we gave the name Malhado (misfortune.) The people we found there are large and well formed. They have no arms but bows and arrows, in the use of which they are very skillful. They have their under lip bored and wear in it a piece of cane the breadth of half a finger. Their women are accustomed to great toil.

23

These people love their children more than any other people in the world, and treat them with the greatest gentleness. When a son dies the parents and kindred weep, and so does everybody else. The wailing for him continues a whole year. They begin before dawn every day, the parents first, and after them the whole town. They do the same at noon and at sunset. After a year of mourning has passed, the funeral rites are performed.

They mourn in this manner for all the dead except the aged. For these they show no regret. They say their season has passed, that they have no pleasure, and that while they live they only occupy the earth and take food from the young people. Their custom is to bury all the dead, except such persons as have been physicians. These they burn.

When they are sick they send for a doctor. He cures by blowing his breath and laying his hands upon them. After he has applied the remedy they give him not only all they have themselves, but seek among their relatives for more to give. The doctor sometimes makes a small cut over the seat of the pain and then sucks the wound. They also make cauteries (burns) with fire. This is a remedy held in high repute by them, and I have tried it on myself and found it beneficial. After burning the sick man they blow on the spot, and then the patient thinks that he is relieved.

The men in all of this region go naked. The women cover part of their bodies with wool that grows on trees. The damsels dress themselves with deerskins.

These people have a custom of weeping half an hour when they meet or when they go visiting. The weeping over, the one that is visited rises and gives the other everything that he has, and the guest accepts it. After a little while the visitor carries the gift away, often going without saying a word.

PART TWO - INDIANS OF THE INTERIOR

Castillo and Stephen went inland. The people there are all good archers. They have fine forms, although they are not so large as those we left near the coast.

Roots of two or three kinds are their principal food, and they hunt for them over the face of all the country. The roots are hard to dig. They require roasting two days, and then many of them are very bitter. Occasionally they kill a deer, and at times catch fish; but the quantity of food thus obtained is so small and the hunger so great that they eat spiders, the eggs of ants, worms, lizards, salamanders, snakes, and poisonous vipers. They also eat earth and wood, and I honestly think that if there were stones in their country they would eat them. They save the bones of the fishes, snakes, and other animals which they consume, so that they may afterwards beat them together and eat the powder.

The women toil very hard and do a great deal of labor. Of the whole twenty-four hours they have only six of the night for repose. The rest of the night they pass in heating the ovens to bake the roots which they eat. At daybreak they begin to dig the roots, bring wood and water to their houses, and prepare other things that may be necessary.

The majority of the people are great thieves; for, though they are free to divide with each other, on turning the head, even a son and a father will steal from one another. They are great liars, and also great drunkards, which they become from drinking a certain liquor.

These Indians are so used to running that with out rest or fatigue they can follow a deer from morning till night. In this way they kill many of them. They pursue them until tired down and then overtake them in the race. Their houses are of matting placed upon four hoops. They move every two or three days to look for food, carrying their houses on their backs.

They are a merry people, considering the hunger they suffer, for they never cease their festivities. They plant nothing for food. To them the happiest time of the year is the season of eating prickly pears, for then they are hungry no longer, but eat day and night, and

25

pass all the time in dancing. They squeeze out the juice of the pears, open them, and set them to dry. When dry they are packed in baskets like figs. The peel is beaten to powder.

Inland there are many deer, birds, and beasts other than those I have spoken of. Cattle come as far as the seacoast from a northerly direction, and range through a tract of more than four hundred leagues.

Three times I have seen them and eaten of their meat. To my judgment the flesh is finer and fatter than that of this country. I think they are about the size of cattle in Spain. They have small horns like the cows of Morocco. Their hair is very long and flocky like Merino wool. Some are tawny, others black. Of the skins of those not full grown the Indians make blankets, and of the larger ones they make shoes and bucklers. Throughout the whole region over which they run the people live upon them, distributing a vast number of hides into the interior country.

Discussion

1. Describe the mourning customs of the Indians of Malhado; their methods of hunting deer.
2. Why did not the Indians mourn the death of old people?
3. What do you suppose it was that Cabeza de Vaca called "wool that grows on trees?"
4. Was Indian life in early Texas easy and comfortable?
5. Compare it with that described in Cooper's Leather Stocking Tales.

Coronado's March Across Texas
by Pedro de Castañeda, 1541

Part One

Coronado was a Spaniard who had come from Mexico to find the famed "Seven Cities of Cibola," whose streets were said to be paved with gold. After finding the cities, but no gold, he pushed on in search of another country called Quivira, about which the Indians told wonderful stories. During the march, described here, the party very probably went through a large portion of Texas. Before turning back they wandered as far as Kansas, but found there only a miserable village of tents.

Castañeda, the writer of this account, was with the company. The story told herein by "The Turk" is an example of the tales by which the early Spaniards were so often misled.

27

While they were making these discoveries, some Indians came to Cibolo (in New Mexico) from a village called Cicuye, seventy leagues east of this province. Among them was a captain (chief) whom our men called Whiskers, because he wore a long moustache. He was a tall, well-built young fellow, with a fine figure. They brought presents of tanned hides, shields, and head-pieces, which were very gladly accepted. The general gave them in return some glass dishes and a number of pearls and little bells which they prized highly, because they had never seen such things before. They described some animals which, from a picture that one of them had painted on his skin, appeared to be cows, although from the hides this did not seem possible, because the hair was woolly and snarled.

The general was much relieved to hear that the country was growing better. He reached Cicuye, a very strong village four stories high. The people came out with signs of joy to welcome Alvarado and their own captain, and escorted them into the town with drums and pipes, something like flutes. They made many presents of cloth and of turquoises, which are very plentiful in that region.

The Spaniards enjoyed themselves here for several days. They talked with an Indian slave, a native of the country toward Florida, the region discovered by De Soto. They called this Indian the Turk, because he looked like one. He said that in his country there was a river two leagues wide running through a level plain. In it there were fish as large as horses.

Upon it floated many immense boats with sails, each boat having more than twenty rowers on a side. The captains of these boats sat under awnings at the stern, and on the prow of each there perched a great golden eagle. The ruler of the country, he said, took his afternoon nap under a large tree on which hung a great number of little gold bells, that put him to sleep as they swung in the air.

He said also that in his country everyone had his ordinary dishes made of wrought plate, and that the jugs and bowls were of gold. He called gold acochis. For the present he was believed, because of the ease with which he told his story, and because he knew gold and silver very well, and did not care anything about other metals.

There were some in the army, however, who already distrusted the Turk. A Spaniard named Cervantes, who had charge of him during the siege, solemnly swore that he had seen him talking with the Devil in a pitcher of water. He also said that while he had him under lock, so that no one could speak to him, the Turk had asked what Christians had been killed by the people of Tiguex (where a fight had occurred.) When told "nobody," he answered: "You lie! Five Christians are dead, including a captain."

Cervantes knew that this was true, and he confessed it, so as to find out who had told him about it. But the Turk said he knew it all by himself, and that he did not need to be told. It was on account of this incident that we watched him and caught him speaking to the Devil in the pitcher, as I have said.

Part Two

The army left Tiguex on the 5th of May, and, taking Whiskers with them, proceeded toward the plains, which are on the other side of the mountains.

The general sent Diego Lopez with ten companions lightly equipped and a guide to go at full speed toward the sunrise for two days. They came across many cattle, and those who were on the advance guard killed a large number. As the cattle fled they trampled one another in their haste. When they came to a ravine so many fell into it that they filled it up, and the rest crossed over them. The men who were chasing them on horseback also fell in among the cattle before they noticed where they were going. Three of the horses that fell in, all saddled and idled, were lost sight of completely.

The general sent Maldonado, with his company, forward from here. He traveled four days and reached an extensive ravine like those of Colima, in the bottom of which he found a large settlement of people. Cabeza de Vaca had passed through this place.

While the army was resting here a storm came up one afternoon with a very high wind and hail. In a short space of time a great quantity of hailstones as big as bowls or bigger fell as thick as raindrops. In places they covered the ground two or three spans or more deep. There was not a horse that did not break away, except two or three which the negroes protected by holding large sea nets over them. Some of them dashed up the sides of the ravine and were brought down only with great difficulty. The hail broke many tents, battered many helmets, wounded many of the horses, and broke all the gourds and the crockery of the army. This was no small loss, because they do not have any crockery nor raise gourds in this region. Neither do they sow corn, nor eat bread; but instead they eat fruit and raw meat—or meat only half cooked.

The people here are called Querechos and Teyas. They travel like the Arabs, with troops of dogs loaded with tents and tent poles. The loads are fastened to Moorish pack saddles with girths. When a load becomes disarranged, the dogs howl, calling some one to fix them right. They are a kind people, are not cruel, and are faithful friends.

They are able to make themselves very well understood by means of signs. They eat raw flesh and drink blood, but do not eat human flesh. They dry the meat they eat in the sun, cutting it thin like a leaf.

When it is dry they grind it like meal to keep it, and make a sort of sea soup of it to eat. They season it with fat, which they always try to secure when they kill a cow. They cut the hide of a cow open at the back and pull it off at the joints, using a flint as large as a finger, tied in a little stick. They do this with as much ease as if working with a good iron tool, and their quickness is something worth seeing. They sharpen the flint with their own teeth.

Discussion

1. What was the object of Coronado's march across Texas?
2. What presents were given by the people of Cicuye to the Spaniards?
3. Describe their musical instruments.
4. What kind of precious stones did they give to the Spaniards?
5. Describe the habits of the Indians seen by the Spaniards while on the plains.

La Salle at an Indian Reception
By Henri Joutel, 1685

*In the spring of 1682 La Salle left Canada and explored the
Mississippi River. He then returned to France and got permission from the king, Louis XIV., to make a settlement at the
mouth of the river. On his way back a storm blew him out of
his course and he landed on the coast of Texas, near the present
town of Matagorda. Joutel, who writes this account, was one
of La Salle's Officers.*

La Salle noticed on the bank of the river a large
tree that he thought would do to make a canoe. He
sent seven or eight men to cut it down. Some hours
later we were surprised to see two of the men running
up, all out of breath and nearly frightened to death.
They said that a band of savages had almost captured
them, and that they believed that their companions
had been taken. At this news La Salle ordered us to
seize our arms and go to see about it.

The Indians were coming towards us, but when they
saw us marching along, all armed and with the drum
beating, they turned round and seemed about to run
away. They thought we were going to fight with them.
As soon as La Salle understood this, he had some of
us lay down our arms. After doing so we started toward them and made signs for them to come to us.
When they saw that we were now unarmed, they also
laid aside their weapons and came to meet us. They
greeted us in their own way. They would strike their
breasts and then rub their hands over our breasts and
arms. They made signs of friendship, and by holding

their hands on their hearts they showed us that they were very glad to see us. We returned their salutation in somewhat the same way.

After a little while we again took the road to camp. Six or seven chiefs went with us, and La Salle ordered some of our men to stay with the Indians as hostages. When we arrived La Salle had the chiefs sit down and gave them something to eat and drink.

Then he tried to talk with them and find out something about the Mississippi River, but he could not understand anything they said. They soon showed that they wanted to leave, so La Salle gave them some hatchets and a few trinkets, and they departed, very happy over their presents.

We found that the Indians had taken our men to their village, about a league and a half away, and La Salle determined to go and look for them. We found their village built on a hill. There were about fifty wigwams covered with rush mats and dried buffalo hides. They were built of large poles, bent in the shape of staves. Upon our arrival, after taking La Salle to the cabin of the principal chief, they wanted to lead us around to their huts, but we had been warned not to separate, so we remained with La Salle.

We saw many women. They were all nude, except for a skin tied round their waists and hanging to the knees. They had some good features, but were not very handsome. The men were entirely naked.

The women brought us some fresh meat and porpoise. I was amazed to see how they cut the meat. They put their feet on it and held it with one hand while they cut it with the other. One does not need

33

to be very polite with people of such manners. They brought us many pieces of porpoise to take back to camp, but in spite of this kind reception we soon took our leave.

Some days after this, seeing a wigwam near the shore of a lake, we approached and found in it an old woman. She started to run away when she saw us, but we caught her and made her understand that we would not hurt her. She returned to the wigwam, where we found several pitchers of water. This we drank. In a little while we saw a canoe coming, and in it were two women and a boy. They landed, and seeing that we had not harmed the old woman, they came up and embraced us in a peculiar way.

They blew on our ears, and told us by signs that their people had gone hunting. A few minutes later seven or eight Indians appeared. It is probable that they had hidden in the weeds when they first saw us coming. They saluted us the same way that the women had done, and this made us laugh. After staying with them a short while, we returned to camp.

34

Discussion

1. How was La Salle received by the Indians in Texas?
2. Describe the appearance of the village that he visited.
3. What did the Indians have to eat?
4. Compare the Indians seen by La Salle with those seen by Cabeza de Vaca and Coronado.

Life at Fort St. Louis
By Henri Joutel, 1685-87

After landing in Texas La Salle built forts to protect his party from the Indians while he was hunting for the Mississippi. A temporary fort was first built on the bay shore, but later a more substantial one was built several miles inland on the Lavaca River.

When Beaujeu was gone, it occurred to us to build a kind of fort, so that we could defend ourselves and the things saved from the wreck of the ship from the attacks of the Indians. We built the fort of pieces of timber, planks, and other material taken from the wrecked ship. When the work was well under way, La Salle determined to take a number of men and look for a suitable place to make a settlement and plant corn and other grain which had been brought along. After doing this he intended to try to find out something about the Mississippi, and see whether or not it flowed into this bay (Matagorda.)

35

While La Salle was preparing some canoes which had been taken from the Indians, we made an oven out of the clay that we found there. This served very well. We had no bricks, because those brought from Haiti were buried in the hold of the ship that was wrecked. Along with them were our bullets and cannon, the most of our lead, the millstones, the anvil, a large part of our iron and steel, and several cases of arms—both muskets and pistols—besides fourteen or fifteen tons of salt and other merchandise which had been brought along.

When the canoes were ready, La Salle chose forty or fifty men to go with him. He left the command of the fort to me, and to Le Gros he gave the duty of distributing the rations. About a hundred or a hundred and twenty persons remained in the fort. Some of them died every day of scurvy, home-sickness, and other ills. There seemed to be a curse upon our mechanics.

During La Salle's absence I occupied myself in finishing the fort and putting it in a condition to withstand the Indians who often came prowling around us, howling like wolves and dogs. Three or four musket shots usually put them to flight. But it happened one night that six or seven shots were fired, and La Salle, who was not far from us, heard them. He was worried, and came back with seven or eight men, but found everything all right.

He told us that he had found a beautiful place, good for sowing and planting all kinds of grain, and abounding in buffaloes and wild fowls. He said that he wanted to build a fort farther inland. For this purpose he ordered me to gather up the timber that the sea cast on the beach, and square as much of it as I could get. He then returned to the camp where he had left his men, and I began to square the logs on the shore.

One day I noticed that the water was bubbling up, and found that it was caused by some kind of fish jumping about. I had a net brought to me, and we caught an enormous quantity. Among them were cat-fish, mullets, and some others about the size of a herring. For several days we had good cheer with them. We often fished in this way, and the fish were very useful to us for food.

By good luck we also discovered that, in the little salt-water pools scattered around, salt was made by the sun. I saw that a white scum was formed on the water, and every two days I had this skimmed off. It proved to be very white and very good salt. I collected a great deal of it, and it also was very useful to us.

Towards the middle of July the bark *La Belle* came to anchor near our camp. It brought orders from La Salle. He instructed me to make a raft, if possible, of the timber that I had squared, but if this could not be done I was to bury in the sand both the logs and the planks of which the fort was built, in order to conceal from the Spanish our presence in the country. We began the raft, but the weather became so stormy that I had to abandon the work. We took to pieces what had been put together, and hid the timber from the Indians as well as we could in the sand. We then joined La Salle where he had resolved to make his new settlement.

Here I was astonished to find everything in such bad condition. The seed and grain that had been planted had almost all either been ruined by the drought or eaten by animals. Several men were dead. A number were sick. There was no shelter except a little square place staked in, where the powder and some casks of brandy were kept. Everything was in a miserable way.

It was necessary to build a fort, but it was not easy to find the timber. A league up the country there was a little wood, where some could be got, but we had neither wagons nor horses to haul it. Nevertheless, La Salle sent some men there to go to work.

Trees were cut down and squared. Some of them were dragged to camp over the grass and weeds that covered the prairie, but later we used a gun carriage to haul them. This labor was so hard that even the strongest men were exhausted. The hard work and scant food caused some of the men to become ill. I suggested to La Salle that it would be better to go after the timber that we had squared on the sea shore. There was a good deal of it, and it could have been brought by water without tiring the men, but, as he had said a number of times before, he wanted no advice. So the work was continued, and many men died; but finally enough timber was hauled and dragged to the place to build the fort.

La Salle now desired to go in search of the Mississippi. He placed me in command during his absence, and gave me an inventory of everything in the fort. There were eight cannons, two hundred fire locks, as many cutlasses, a hundred barrels of powder, three thousand pounds of musket balls, about three hundred pounds of other lead, some bars of iron, twenty bundles of iron to make nails, and some tools, such as hatchets. As for provisions, there were only twenty casks of meal, a cask and a half of wine, three fourths of a cask of brandy, some hogs, a cock and a hen.

Knowing that idleness often occasions restlessness and impatience, I tried in every way to keep the men busy. Some of them I set to cutting down the bushes around the fort, others to felling trees that obstructed the view, and still others to mowing the grass, so that fresh grass might grow. At night I made them amuse themselves with singing and dancing.

Discussion

1. Where was La Salle's first settlement made?
2. Why did he decide to move?
3. Locate Fort St. Louis.
4. Describe the building of the fort.
5. What supplies did the fort contain?
6. Upon what did the inmates live?
7. Why were they kept always busy?
8. How did they get timber to build?
9. How did they get salt?

Fatal Search for the Mississippi
By Henri Joutel, 1687

La Salle decided to make another attempt to find the Mississippi River, and he wanted me to go with him. He began to provide by degrees what he thought he would need on the expedition. I had two sheets, and these he took to make clothes. We also made clothes of the sails of La Belle. Besides this, Duhaut had some linen, and La Salle distributed it among several persons.

On the 12th of January, 1687, seventeen of us set out. To our friends in the fort we said farewell as affectionately as if we had foreseen that we should never see each other again. Father Zenobius told me that he had never in his life before been so deeply affected by a parting.

The first of March we met some Indians. On a former trip La Salle had hid some corn and beans two or three leagues from this place, and, since our provisions were now running short, he thought it best to send for them. He described the place, and ordered Duhaut, Hiens, and Liotot, the surgeon, to go with his Indian guide and his own servant, Saget, to get them. But they found them all rotted and ruined.

On their return they came across two buffaloes, and the Indian killed them. They sent the servant back to tell La Salle that they would dry the flesh, and that he could send horses for it. La Salle accordingly ordered Moranger and De Male to go with the servant and bring back a load of the meat immediately.

When Moranger arrived he found that they were smoking both of the buffaloes, but that they were not yet dry enough. The marrow bones and other parts that could not be saved had been laid aside to be roasted. Moranger found fault with this. In a great passion he seized both the meat and the bones, and declared that they should not eat as much of them as they had expected.

These men already had other causes of complaint against Moranger, and this behavior made them very angry. They decided upon a bloody revenge—the murder of Moranger, the servant, and the Indian. They waited until night, when the unfortunate wretches had eaten supper and were asleep. Then Liotot, the inhuman executioner, took an ax and began with Moranger. He crushed his head with many blows of the ax, and then did the same with the servant and the Indian, while his fellow villains stood on guard ready to shoot if any of them resisted.

This massacre did not satisfy them. To save themselves from punishment they decided that they would have to kill La Salle. But between them and us there was a river which was swollen and difficult to cross, so they delayed during the 18th and 19th. La Salle, in the meantime, became very uneasy about Moranger and resolved to go and look for him.

When he came near the camp of the murderers he saw some buzzards fluttering around and fired a shot at them. The murderers heard the shot and concluded that it was La Salle coming after them. They prepared to waylay him. Duhaut and Larcheveque crossed the river. Then Duhaut went ahead and hid himself in the high weeds to wait for him to pass. La Salle suspected nothing, and did not even load his gun again. He saw Larcheveque a good way off, and immediately asked him about his nephew, Moranger. Larcheveque told him that he was down the river, and at the same moment Duhaut shot La Salle through the head. He dropped dead on the spot, without speaking a word. This is the exact account of this murder as it was soon afterwards told to me by Father Anastasius.

Discussion

1. Why did La Salle want to find the Mississippi?
2. How many expeditions did he make in search of it?
3. How many men accompanied La Salle on his second expedition?
4. How many returned with him?
5. State the events leading up to La Salle's murder.
6. From whom did Joutel hear the details of La Salle's murder?
7. Upon what did the French government base its claim to Texas?
8. Who wrote these three stories about La Salle?
9. Was he a good witness?

The Spaniards Find Fort St. Louis
by Damian Manzanet, 1689

The stories told in this and the next three pieces are parts of a letter" written to a friend by Father Manzanet, who went to Texas with the expeditions that he describes. He had charge of the missionary work, and founded the first mission in Texas.

My Dear Don Carlos:

The following is the story for which you ask me, of the discovery of the bay of Espiritu Santo and the river of the Tejas:

Knowing that his Excellency (the viceroy of Mexico) was taking steps to lead to the discovery of the bay of Espiritu Santo, and find out whether any Frenchmen were there, I tried to learn from the Indians coming from the interior whether they knew where there dwelt white men like the Spaniards. In time I learned that there were some. He who told me was an Indian whom I had converted a little before. Just at this time there came another Indian, of the Quems nation, who told me that he had been in the very houses of the French. There were many of them, he said, including women. They were well armed, and had some very large fire-arms (referring to the cannons). On my asking whether he were well acquainted with the country, he replied that, if I wished, he would take me to the place.

At this time Captain Alonso de Leon became captain of the presidio of Coahuila. Now, before going out to his presidio he came to Mission Caldera, where

I was living. I told him what had passed between the Indians and me, and tried to persuade him that he ought to go to the bay of Espiritu Santo. He asked me whether I had any proof that the story was true. So I called the Indian by the name of John, captain of the Papul nation, and he said that in a village of heathen Indians, some sixty leagues away, there was one of the white men that he had mentioned as living in the interior.

I notified Captain de Leon, who, with twelve men, went and brought the Frenchman to Caldera. He was painted like the Indians, old, and naked. His name was John Francis So-and-so, and, by his own account, he was a native of Cheblie in New France.

The viceroy now ordered Captain de Leon to go to the bay. For the expedition forty men went from the presidio of Viscaya, and forty others went from the New Kingdom of Leon. Three companies were formed, with Captain de Leon as commander. We left Coahuila on the twenty-sixth of March, 1689.

Now, the old Frenchman, who accompanied us, took occasion to say that the French settlement was not in the place to which the Indian guides were taking us. On the way he tried several times to make our two Indians desert us, or say that it was very far, and that we would not be able to cross the rivers which were on the way. I was so sorry that the Frenchman was allowed to speak that I grew annoyed.

We arrived at a stream of very good drinking water, and the two Indians said to me: "Lower down on the bank of this stream are the houses of the French. They must be about three leagues off."

Then the old Frenchman saw that there was no help, and that we were certain to come upon the village. He then said: "Sir, now I know very well, yea, very well, that the houses are on this little river."

We started the next morning, and three leagues off we found the village of the Frenchmen on the bank of the stream. We arrived at about eleven in the forenoon, and found six small houses, built with poles, plastered with mud, and roofed over with buffalo hides. There was another large house where pigs were kept; and a wooden fort made from the hulk of a wrecked vessel. The fort had one lower room which was used as a chapel for saying mass, and three other rooms below. Above the three rooms was an upper story serving for a storehouse. In this we found some six loads of iron and steel (not counting scattered pieces), also eight small guns and three swivels made of iron, the largest guns being for a charge of about six pounds of shot. The guns and one swivel were buried, and Captain de Leon carried off two of the swivels. There was a great lot of shattered weapons, broken by the Indians—firelocks, carbines, cutlasses—but they had not left the cannon, only one being found. We found two unburied bodies, which I interred, setting up a cross over the grave. There were also many torn-up books and a number of dead pigs.

These Frenchmen had a piece of land fenced in with stakes where they sowed a little corn and had an asparagus bed. This place affords no advantages of situation, for good drinking water is very far off, and timber still further. The water of the stream is very brackish, so much so that in five days during which

45

the camp was pitched there, all the horses sickened. The Indians dig wells for drinking water.

After exploring the bay we returned to the main body of our party, which we had left in the village. The next day we bent the large iron bars, making them up into bundles in order to carry them with ease. We found the Indians with the reply to the letter which we had written to the Frenchmen. They said that we should wait for them, and that another Frenchman was further on, for whom they were waiting, in order that they all might come together. As to the fort, Captain de Leon would not have it burned down, and it remained where it was.

The next day we set out on our return trip to the Guadalupe River. When we got half way, since we saw that the Frenchmen did not come, Captain de Leon, with twenty-five men, went to the settlement where they were, and the main party went on as far as the Guadalupe River, where it remained waiting three days. Two Frenchmen came naked, except for antelope skins, and with their faces, breasts, and arms painted like the Indians. With them came the governor of the Tejas and eight of his Indians.

Through that day and night I tried my utmost to show all possible consideration to the governor, giving him two horses and the blanket in which I slept. Speaking Spanish and using one of the Frenchmen as an interpreter, I exhorted the governor that his people should become Christians, adding that if he wished I would go to his country. Soon the governor said he would very willingly take me there, and I promised that I would be there in the following year at the time of sowing corn. The governor seemed well pleased, and I was still more so, seeing the harvest to be reaped in those lands where they know not God.

The next day was the day of the Holy Cross—the 3d of May. After mass the governor of the Tejas left for his home and we for this place.

Discussion

1. What part had Father Manzanet in getting up the expedition to Texas?
2. How did he learn the whereabouts of the French?
3. How many Frenchmen were in the expedition?
4. How many Frenchmen did they find?
5. Compare the description of the French settlement with that given by Joutel.
6. Describe the visit of the Tejas chief to the Spaniards.

47

The Destruction of Fort St. Louis
by Damian Manzanet, 1690

His Excellency decided that a second expedition should be undertaken to the bay of Espiritu Santo. He ordered that Captain de Leon should go as commander, and take with him a hundred and ten soldiers, one hundred and fifty long guns, twelve hundred weight of powder, and three hundred weight of shot.

They were to inspect the bay and learn whether there were any Frenchmen left of those who used to live there, or whether others had recently arrived. The wooden fort built by the French was to be burnt down, and from the bay Captain de Leon was to communicate with the governor of the Tejas, to find out whether he would be willing to have the minister of the gospel enter into his territory.

I remarked that I would take along three priests for the Tejas, myself being the fourth, besides two for the mission of San Salvador, which is on the way. This made a total of six priests to be sent immediately by the college. In the event of the Tejas receiving the faith, the college was to send whatever others would be required.

His Excellency bade me make a note of what I needed to take along. I replied that for the present I only wanted wine for the masses, a wafer box, and wax. As to other necessaries, such as vestments, I could get them myself. It was determined that the journey should take place after Christmas, so when the Christmas feast was over his Excellency dispatched Captain

48

Francisco Martinez with twenty mules laden with wine, wax, and so on, clothing for distribution among the Indians, and six loads of tobacco. At the college of the Holy Cross at Queretaro, with the priests who were to accompany me, I awaited him.

We left Coahuila for the Tejas on the third day of the Easter feast, March 28, 1690. When we left the twenty soldiers from Viscaya had not yet arrived. The forty from Zacatecas were for the most part tailors, carpenters, masons, miners, in short, none of them could catch the horses on which they were to ride that day, for when they had once let them go they could manage them no longer. Besides, we had saddles that could not have been worse.

Twenty of us reached the fort built by the Frenchmen. The rest remained with the horses by the Guadalupe River. We saw no trace of Frenchmen having been there during our absence, all being as we had left it the year before, except that there were signs that the Indians had dwelt there. I myself set fire to the fort, and as there was a high wind—the wood, by the way, was from the Frenchmen's sloop, which had sunk on entering the bay—in half an hour the fort was in ashes. This was at the hour of noon; afterwards we went down to the coast of the bay, all along the banks of the rivulet by which the Frenchmen passed in and out of the bay with their barges and canoes.

After we had arrived, some of the soldiers of the Kingdom of Leon said that they wished to bathe, in order to be able to tell that they had bathed in the sea. This was thought such a wonderful thing that they carried away flasks of sea water, and later, in their own country of Monterey, it was considered a great favor to taste it.

Discussion

1. What reasons are given for de Leon's second expedition to Fort St. Louis?
2. Describe the military equipment of the party.
3. What instructions were given to the captain?
4. How many priests accompanied the soldiers?
5. What kind of supplies were taken for the missions?
6. How were they carried?
7. Describe what the Spaniards did after arriving at the fort.
8. Were such expeditions all hardship?

The Chief's Household
by Damian Manzanet, 1690

This extract gives an excellent description of an Indian chief's household arrangements. It also illustrates the early Spanish custom of calling things in Indian society by names taken from civilized life. Thus they called the chief a "governor," and his servants "pages."

There came into that region an Indian who was thoroughly acquainted with the road into the country of the Tejas, and he showed us the way. As soon as the governor saw me, he came forward to embrace me. We sat down to talk by signs—this being the most usual mode of communication in those regions.

He produced a small sack of powdered tobacco, of the kind which they grow, and another small sack of white pinóle (parched corn, ground and crushed) of very good quality. That night it was arranged to provide the governor with garments, in order that he might enter his village clothed, so that his people might see how highly we thought of him.

The governor expressed a desire to take us home with him and said that we might live in his house, in which, he said, there was room for all. After dinner we, the priests, discussed what should be our conduct on visiting at the governor's. My opinion was that we four priests should go on foot, carrying our staffs, which bore a holy crucifix, and singing the Litany of Our Lady, and that a lay-brother who was with us should carry in front a picture of the Blessed Virgin, bearing it high on his lance, like a banner.

51

We came to the governor's house, where we found a number of Indians—men, women, and children. Kneeling, we concluded the Litany, and blessed the house. Soon the governor and the other Indians came up to kiss my robe, and the former bade us enter and look at his house. It is built of stakes thatched over with grass. It is about twenty yards high, is round, and has no windows, daylight entering through the door only. In the middle of the house is the fire, which is never extinguished by day or by night. Over the door on the inner side there is a little mound of pebbles very prettily arranged. Placed around one half of the house, inside, are ten beds, each of which consists of a rug made of reeds laid on four forked sticks. Over the rug they spread buffalo skins on which they sleep. At the head and foot of the bed is attached another carpet forming a sort of arch, which, lined with a brilliantly colored piece of reed matting, makes what bears some resemblance to a very pretty alcove.

In the other half of the house, where there are no beds, there are some shelves about two yards high. On them are arranged large round baskets made of reeds, in which they keep their corn, nuts, acorns, beans, etc. There is also a row of very large earthen pots like our earthen jars. These are used only to make the atole (a gruel of pounded corn) when there is a large crowd on the occasion of some ceremony. On the shelves are also six wooden mortars for pounding the corn in rainy weather. When it is fair, they grind the corn in the courtyard.

After a little while they brought out to each of us in the courtyard a small wooden bench very skillfully fashioned, and we sat down there, for the yard was bright and cool. Next they brought us a lunch. It consisted of tamales, nuts, pinole very well prepared, and a large crock full of corn stewed with beans.

Soon I noticed, outside the yard, opposite the door of the governor's house, a long building in which no inmates could be seen. I asked who lived in it or what purpose it served, and was told that the captains were lodged in it when the governor called them to a meeting. On the other side of the yard I saw yet another and smaller house also vacant. Upon my inquiring about this one they told me that in it the pages of the captains were lodged. There is a law providing that each captain shall bring his page when the governor assembles them, and this custom is observed. As soon as the pages arrive they are lodged in this house, where for each one is laid a large, brightly colored reed mat. They sleep on this mat with a bolster made of painted reeds for a pillow. The governor provides them with food until he sends them home. When they return home, each one carries with him his mat and pillow.

The following are the domestic arrangements in the governor's house. Each week ten Indian women do the housework. Every day at sunrise they come laden with firewood, sweep out the courtyard and the house, carry water from a brook some distance away, and grind corn for the food. All the women go home for the night, returning to the governor's house next morning.

I noticed a little wooden bench in front of the fire. The Indians admonished me not to sit upon it, lest

53

I should die. Of course I was curious to learn what mystery there was connected with it, and they told me that no one but their lord, the governor, might sit upon that stool.

Discussion

1. Describe the Texas chief's welcome to Father Manzanet.
2. How was the chief's house built?
3. Draw a diagram of it.
4. Describe the furniture.
5. What other buildings were near the chief's house?
6. Describe the customs with regard to "pages."
7. Describe the house-keeping arrangements of the chief.
8. Were these Indians superstitious?

Founding Mission San Francisco
by Damian Manzanet, 1690

In this piece Father Manzanet tells how he founded Mission San Francisco, the first mission ever planted in Texas.

It seemed to me inadvisable that the priests should live in the governor's house, on account of the number of Indians, men and women, who went in and out at all times. Using the Frenchman as an interpreter, I told the governor, with many kind expressions, that his house was very fine, and that I heartily appreciated his desire to have the priests in his household, but that since we had to build a house for the celebration of the masses, it might be well to build likewise a dwelling for the priests, because they must live near the church. Thereupon the governor said that we could build the house I asked for in the most suitable place, that he would show us the village, and that I might choose the spot.

55

The next morning I went out with Captain de Leon a little way, and found a delightful spot close to the brook, with fine woods, and plum trees like those in Spain. Soon afterwards, on the same day, they began to fell trees and cart the wood, and within three days we had a roomy dwelling and a church wherein to say mass. Very reverently we set a high cross of carved wood in front of the church.

On the eve of Corpus Christi mass was sung. Before mass we had a procession with the holy sacrament exposed. A large number of Indians were assembled for we had notified them the day before. The soldiers had been given leave to fire as many salutes as they could during the procession, at the elevation (of the cross), and at the close of mass. After mass we hoisted the royal standard, which bore on one side the picture of Christ crucified, and on the other that of the Virgin of Guadalupe.

When the church and the dwelling intended for the priests had been finished, they carried into these buildings all that was to be left for the priests, and on the morning of the first of June, a week from the feast of Corpus Christi, we consecrated the church and celebrated mass. After singing a hymn of thanksgiving, the soldiers fired a royal salute. The church and village were dedicated to our Holy Father St. Francis.

After dinner on the same day our company left the place, to return to Coahuila, but I remained until the next day, when I went to overtake the others on the way. The night before I left the place I called the governor and told him to remember that he must take care of the fathers who remained there, and try to make his people respect them and receive the Christian doctrine. I told him the fathers would not take anything away from them, nor ask them for anything, but, rather, would help them whenever they were able.

The governor replied: "I shall take care of the fathers, so that, when you return, they will have no complaint to bring against me; they are perfectly safe, and may remain."

It was arranged that three soldiers recommended by me should remain there. They were willing to do so, and were quite content. Captain de Leon left for the soldiers nine of the king's horses, some firelocks, a barrel of powder and some shot; and for the priests he left twenty-six loads of flour, twenty cows, two yoke of oxen, ploughs with ploughshares, axes, spades, and other little things.

On the 2nd day of June we took our departure, and the priests walked with us a little way out of the village. Then we took leave of one another with many tears of joy and gladness, for these men did not sorrow at being left behind; nay, they gave thanks to God for having merited such grace as to be called to save the souls of the heathen.

Discussion

1. Describe the ceremony with which the priests approached the chief's village.
2. Why did they observe so much ceremony?
3. Describe the steps that were taken in establishing the mission. How long did it take to build the house and the church?
4. How many soldiers were left to guard the mission?
5. What supplies were left?
6. Tell about the writer of the last three stories.

St. Denis in Texas
by Andre Joseph Penicaut, 1714

In 1714 the French governor of Louisiana, Cadillac, sent an expedition to open up trade across Texas with the Spanish of Mexico. The leader chosen for the undertaking was a shrewd Frenchman named St. Denis. The story of his journey from Mobile to Texas and thence to Mexico is here told by Peni-caut, who was with the party. The result of the expedition was to frighten the Spanish into a new attempt to occupy eastern Texas which they had deserted in 1693.

St. Denis, a brave and enterprising officer, was called to Mobile by Governor Cadillac. After his arrival, the governor made him a proposition to go to Natchitoches, and from thence by land to Mexico, to establish commercial relations with that country. St. Denis accepted the proposal. He took about two thousand dollars' worth of merchandise from the public stores, and loaded it in five canoes. Provided with a passport to the Spanish governor, he set out from the fort at Mobile Bay, accompanied by twenty men, of whom I was one, and proceeded on the expedition to Mexico. We stopped at Biloxi, where St. Denis resides. Here we remained some time for the purpose of collecting all the Natchitoches Indians we could. We succeeded in obtaining about thirty in addition to those we already had.

We ascended the Mississippi to Pass Manchac, where we killed fifteen buffaloes. The next day we landed again and killed eight more buffaloes and as many deer. We then left the Mississippi and proceeded with our merchandise to the Red River.

As soon as St. Denis arrived at the village of the Natchitoches Indians he assembled the chiefs and told them they must begin to cultivate their lands, and that he was about to distribute to them the corn and grain he had brought for sowing. He said that they would always have the French among them, and that the Indians would have to supply them with food. He advised them to go to work at once, saying that they would have nothing to fear from hostile Indians so long as they continued united among themselves. We distributed among them pick-axes, hoes, and axes. They cut down some trees, and we built with them two houses in their village, one for lodging and one for storing our merchandise.

After remaining here six weeks we set out, on the 23d of August, to explore the Spanish territory. We took with us twelve Frenchmen, and for guides we had thirty Indians. Ten Frenchmen were left to guard the goods in the village, with instructions to keep close watch over them.

I was one of those who accompanied St. Denis. We went to the village of the Assinais by land, because the river above Natchitoches is impeded by timber. During the entire march we lived on the products of our hunting. Our rations consisted of an ear of corn and a piece of buffalo meat. The Assinais were astonished at seeing us, as they had never before seen any French. They had seen only some half naked, half civilized Spaniards, and even these had not visited them for five years past. The Indians chanted the calumet

59

of peace to St. Denis, who gave them presents and employed them as guides in search of the Spaniards.

In their village we found a woman, named Angelica, who had been baptized by the Spanish priests. She spoke Spanish very well, and, as St. Denis was familiar with that language, he employed her as chief interpreter. We took but few provisions with us, as we could not obtain many among the Assinais, and we were compelled again to live by hunting. We went on in this way for one hundred and fifty leagues, and at the end of a month and a half reached the first Spanish village, called El Presidio del Norte, situated on the banks of the Rio Grande.

As soon as we arrived there Don Ramón, a captain of the Spanish cavalry, came to speak with St. Denis, to learn the object of his visit. St. Denis told him that the governor of Louisiana had sent him to open commercial relations with the Spaniards. The captain, who was a man of good sense, replied that he had no authority in the matter, but would write to the governor of Coahuila and give St. Denis an answer as soon as he should get orders from his superior. He then provided lodgings for the soldiers, and invited to his own house St. Denis, accompanied by his servant and myself.

At length the governor sent an officer and twenty-five cavalry to the village where we were with an order to take St. Denis before him. Upon his departure St. Denis told us to await his return in the village. We stayed there over a month, I at the house of the captain, and the soldiers and Indians at their lodgings. At the end of this time we got orders from St. Denis to return to Natchitoches, because the governor, after an examination of St. Denis' passport, had resolved to send him to Mexico, three hundred leagues distant. (He arrived there on the 25th of June and did not return until the following year (1715).

I gave the captain my most sincere thanks for his kindness and hospitality. His name was Don Pedro de Villescas. He had two daughters. One of them, Doña Maria, was afterwards married to St. Denis, on his return from Mexico.

Discussion

1. What was the purpose of St. Denis' journey into Texas?
2. Describe his equipment.
3. His route.
4. How did he treat the Indians at Natchitoches?
5. What did he do when among the Assinais?
6. Who acted as chief interpreter?
7. Who was Doña Maria ?

61

A Pipe of Peace
by Antonio Bonilla, 1716

Upon St. Denis' arrival in Mexico, steps were at once taken to prevent French encroachment upon Spanish soil. An expedition composed of sixty-five persons was organized with Domingo Ramon as commander. St. Denis, who had made friends with the Spaniards, served as guide and interpreter. The expedition entered Texas in 1716, and resulted in the re-establishment of Mission San Francisco and the founding of five others, all within a radius of about fifty miles from Nacogdoches. The following story, telling of some of the interesting things the party did on the way, is from a history of Texas written in 1772 by Antonio Bonilla.

62

St. Denis had gone ahead to let the chief of the Tejas know about the entrance of the Spaniards into his territory. On the 26th of June he came into camp with five captains and twenty-nine Indians. They came on horseback, following St. Denis in single file. Some of them were armed with French guns. As soon as they came into camp they dismounted, leaving their horses and arms with other Indians.

Still in single file, they approached our men, who were awaiting them drawn up in two lines, between which were Captain Ramón and the missionaries. All embraced one another in turn, with especial marks of love and friendship, and after a salute of musketry they went to a hut covered with leafy boughs which the Spaniards had prepared for their reception. There, when all were seated according to rank, the

Indians performed the peace ceremony.

The chief took out a pipe much adorned with white feathers. Filling it with tobacco and lighting it, he smoked it first himself and then required everybody else to smoke it. The rest responded by repeating what he had done. The ceremony ended with a serious speech by the Indian chief, in which, according to St. Denis, who understood perfectly the language of that nation, he told how glad he was that the Spaniards were settling his country.

Afterwards various chiefs and families joined the party and became the subjects of the King. Captain Ramon distributed freely among them the presents which he had brought. He appointed as captain general of those nations a son of the Tejas chief, and named, likewise, the alcaldes and fiscals of each village. Finally, there were founded the four missions of San Francisco, the Immaculate Conception, St. Joseph, and Our Lady of Guadalupe, where more than five thousand persons of the same tongue were gathered together. The most distant of the missions was situated seven leagues from Natchitoches.

63

Discussion

1. Who was commander of the expedition described here?
2. What missions were founded by him?
3. Where do you suppose the Indians had got their horses?
4. Did the Indians seen by de Leon have horses?
5. How did the Indians make peace?
6. What offices did Ramon give the Indians?

Speeches and Presents
by Fr. Juan Antonio de la Peña, 1721

In 1719 the Spanish settlements in eastern Texas were abandoned because of fear of the French. Two years later the Marquis de Aguayo was sent to re-establish them and to build some forts to keep out the French. The following story of the meeting with the Indians on the Neches is by the chaplain of the expedition. It tells of strange Indian habits and of the Spanish custom of giving presents to the natives.

On Wednesday, (July) 30th, there came into camp (on the Neches River) one hundred Indians, including women and children, who lived in Macono, five leagues from where we were. They had belonged to the first mission of San Francisco. Their captain, who is also chief priest of their idols, is blind. Perhaps after he had been captain many years he put out his own eyes, according to a custom of the Indians, in order to become their chief priest. In the natural rhetoric of voice and signs he made a long and most powerful speech to his lordship, expressing the greatest joy at the return of the Spaniards. To show his love for them he said that what he most esteemed was God, the sun, the moon, and the Spaniards he said that neither air, water, earth, nor fire, would serve for this comparison.

The governor answered this speech through the interpreter, Nicolas de los Santos, a soldier who had been with Domingo Ramon on his first expedition to Texas, and who was very well versed in the Indian language and signs. He expressed the warmest appreciation for the chief's affectionate words, and explained His Majesty's purpose in sending so many Spaniards into the country. He said that the object was to bring peace to all this wide province, and to leave it guarded by many Spaniards. He told them that whenever it was necessary many more would be sent to defend them from all their enemies, and that missionaries would come to establish the Catholic faith for the benefit of the Indians.

On Thursday the Indians brought to the governor tamales, watermelons, flowers, pinóle, and beans. His lordship gave all the women coarse cloth, handkerchiefs, and ribbons, to use for dress, and made them presents of glass beads, pocket knives, large knives, hoes, finger rings, mirrors, combs, awls, scissors, steels, and blankets, which they prize very highly.

To the chief he gave a silver headed cane, and a dress indicating rank, according to the custom of the Spaniards. To the chief's wife he gave one each of all the other presents. They were all very much pleased with these things and very grateful for them.

65

A Marquis Builds a Fort
by Fr. Juan Antonio de la Peña, 1721

The fort, or presidio, of Adaes, herein described by La Peña, was one of several built by Aguayo. A careful study of the diagram in connection with this description will give a good idea of a Spanish fortification in Texas. The last paragraph shows the way in which the founding of a mission or the building of a fort was celebrated.

The Marquis now set about choosing a site for a fort. Although he sent explorers through the whole surrounding country, and even went out himself to look it over, he found no place more suitable than the one where he was encamped. This was on the royal Natchitoches road, seven leagues from Natchitoches. All the rest of the country was rough and shaded by woods. But this place had good valleys in which to erect the mission near the fort; there was sufficient land for both the Spaniards and Indians to make their crops; and nearby there was a spring on the side of a hill. On the top of this elevation, which commanded the whole plain, his lordship laid out and began at once to build the fortification. He gave it the form of a hexagon, making each side about fifty-five yards long. He left three bastions unconstructed and made the other three smaller than he had planned. These he placed at alternate corners, so that each commandant's quarters would protect two sides of the fort.

He made these changes in his plan to suit the nature of the land and the few soldiers assigned to the fort.

66

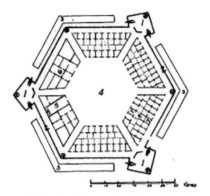

1. The bastions. 2. The palisades.
3. The ditches. 4. The plaza.
5. The church. 6. The stores and
commandant's quarters. 7. Barracks for the officers.

Plan of Presidio de los Adaes

He had only one hundred, and thirty of these were *67*
always occupied in the protection and care of the
horses and flocks. Another reason for reducing the
number and the size of the bastions was that there
were only six cannons to guard the water, which is at
a gunshot's distance.

In building this fortification the greatest task was
to open the space for the foundations, which had to
be done with the crowbar, and to clear the site and its
surroundings of very heavy timber, so that the enemy
may not approach unseen. This will thus put the fort
in better condition for defense.

As there are no stones at the fort, not even small
ones, the palisade of stakes will be strengthened by
a thick wall of adobe. And the ditch which is outside
the fort will be extended around the bastions also. No
pains will be spared to make a well within the plaza.

The living rooms of the missionary fathers are near the church. The stores and the quarters of the commander are in the part of the enclosure next to the church. The barracks in the division at the gate are for the officers. The rest of the barracks, each with its corral, are for the soldiers.

On the day of the Archangel of San Miguel they celebrated in the church the restoration of the mission, which was to be located about a quarter of a league away. On the 12th of October they dedicated the church and the fort, choosing the Holy Virgin as patroness and guardian of the frontier.

These two occasions were celebrated with the greatest display possible. Salutes were fired by the artillery and by the companies that had formed in the plaza of arms. Mass was sung by Doctor Rabal, who had already blessed the church. He took in procession the image of Our Lady of Pilár, whom Father Margil praised in an eloquent sermon.

The affair ended with a splendid banquet at which the fathers and the soldiers were given whisky, and they showed their merriment by various dances and capers.

Discussion

1. Where was Adaes?
2. Mention the desirable features of the site.
3. What materials were used in the construction?
4. Name the parts of the fort.
5. What classes of people were to live within it?

A Description of Mission, 1762

This description of Mission San Antonio de Valero, better known as the Alamo, is part of an official report on the condition of the Texas missions made in 1762. It gives a good idea of a mission settlement.

In this province are some beautiful springs. So great is the volume of water which they send forth, that within a short distance a river of considerable size is formed. This stream, called the San Antonio, runs from north to south. West of it, and one league below the springs, stand the town of San Fernando and the presidio of San Antonio. Across the river on its eastern bank and about two gunshots from the presidio is the mission of San Antonio de Valero. This mission was founded on the first of May, 1718, by order of the most excellent Marquis of Valero. It was the first which the college of the Holy Cross, in its zeal for the salvation of the natives, planted in the province of Texas.

The records show that since its foundation seventeen hundred and ninety-two persons have been baptized. At present there are seventy-six families here, which, counting widows and widowers, orphans and other children, comprise two hundred and seventy-five persons.

The settlement contains a convent fifty yards square, with arcades above and below. In the convent are the living rooms of the religious, the porter's lodge, the dining-room, the kitchen, and the offices. All these

69

rooms are adorned with sacred ornaments and furnished with such articles as are needed by the religious for their own use and for supplying the Indians.

In the second court is a room large enough for four looms. Upon these looms are made coarse cloths, embroidered cotton shawls, blankets, and other common fabrics of wool and cotton needed to supply and properly clothe the Indians. Adjoining this room are two others in which they keep the stock of wool, cotton, combs, skeins, spindles, cards, and other things used by the Indians in making their clothing.

The church of this mission was finished, even to towers and sacristy, but, on account of the stupidity of the builder, it tumbled down. Another, however, of pleasing architecture, is being constructed of hewn stones. For the present a room which was built for a granary serves as a church. In it are an altar with wooden table and steps, a niche containing a sculptured image of St. Anthony, an image of Christ crucified, and another of St. John. All of these are dressed in robes, undergarments, and silken vestments.

A big room is used as the sacristy. In it are kept the large boxes that contain the ornaments. Among these are three covered chalices, two large cups, four communion vessels, a silken case for the cross, a vessel and a sprinkler for holy water, two candlesticks, an incense boat and spoon, a censer, and three holy oil vials. All of these are of silver.

The mission has a well built stone chapel eleven yards long. Among its ornaments is a stone cross two yards high and capped with silver. In the cross are hidden four reliquaries, each containing its own relic.

The altar is adorned with carved and painted images.

There are seven rows of houses for the dwellings of the Indians. They are made of stone and supplied with doors and windows. They are furnished with high beds, chests, metátes, pots, flat earthen pans, kettles, cauldrons, and boilers. With their arched porticoes the houses form a broad and beautiful plaza through which runs a canal skirted by willows and fruit trees, and used by the Indians. To insure a supply of water in case of blockade by the enemy a curbed well has been made.

For the defense of the settlement the plaza is surrounded by a wall. Over the gate is a large tower with its embrasures, three cannons, some firearms, and appropriate supplies.

For cultivating the fields of corn, chile, and beans that are tilled to feed the Indians, and of cotton to clothe them, there are fifty pairs of cart-oxen, thirty of which are driven in-yoke. There are also traces, ploughs, ploughshares, fifty axes, forty pickaxes, twenty-two crowbars, and twenty-five sickles. For hauling stone, wood, and other things there are twelve carts. For carpentering they have the ordinary tools, such as adzes, chisels, planes, picks, hammers, saws, and plummets. For use in repairing their implements they have an anvil, tongs, a screw, mallets, hammers, files, and other things connected with a forge. In the large room where the grain is kept there are at present about eighteen hundred bushels of corn and some beans. These supplies are to feed the Indians.

The mission owns a ranch upon which is a stone house about twenty-five yards long. It has an arched

71

portico, and is divided into three rooms. These are occupied by the families that care for the stock, which consists of one hundred and fifteen gentle horses, one thousand one hundred and fifteen head of cattle, two thousand three hundred sheep and goats, two hundred mares, fifteen jennies, and eighteen saddle mules.

The mission and the ranch have the necessary corrals. For the irrigation of the fields there is a fine main aqueduct.

Discussion

1. Where was the mission San Antonio de Valero situated with reference to the San Antonio River?
2. When was it founded and for whom named?
3. What was the population of the mission settlement at the time this description was written?
4. Name the different buildings described.
5. How were the Indians fed and clothed?
6. Describe the dwellings of the Indians.
7. Describe the stock of farm implements and tools.
8. What kinds of animals were raised on the ranch?

72

PART TWO
The Filibusters

73

To reckless spirits journeying from afar,
'Tis Texas yet presents a polar star.

74

- Edward Siff, 1840

Wild Horse Hunting in Texas
by Peter Ellis Bean, 1801

*Why Philip Nolan came to Texas is not positively known,
but the Spanish authorities feared that he had evil purposes.
A man named Richards, who had been with Nolan, told
the Mexican viceroy that Nolan intended to build a fort
near the Caddo Indians, hunt for mines, catch wild horses,
and, after being joined by men from Kentucky, to conquer
Texas. Bean wrote this narrative about fifteen years after
the Nolan expedition.*

[At Natchez] I got acquainted with a man by the
name of Nolan, who had been for some years trading
with the Spaniards in San Antonio. He told me that
he was going to make another voyage to that country
in October, and entreated me to go along with him. I
readily agreed to go.

Steering a west course through the Mississippi
swamp for the Washita, we were about forty miles
from the river when we met some fifty Spaniards
mounted on horseback and well armed.

They had been sent by the commandant at Washita
to stop us; but, though our number was only twen-
ty-one, they were afraid to attack us. We asked them
their business. They told us they were in pursuit of
some Choctaw Indians who had stolen some horses.
This was false, for they were hunting for our party,
though they were afraid to own it.

In about six days journey we came to Trinity River,
and, crossing it, we found the big, open prairie of that
country. We passed through the plains till we reached

a spring, which we called the Painted Spring, because a rock at the head of it was painted by the Comanche and Pawnee Indians in a peace that was made there by these two nations. We found that the buffalo were getting so scarce that in three days after passing the spring we were forced, in order to sustain life, to eat the flesh of wild horses, which we found in great quantities. For about nine days we were compelled to eat horseflesh, when we arrived at a river called the Brazos. Here we found elk and deer plentiful, some buffalo, and wild horses by thousands. We built a pen and caught about three hundred horses.

After some days the Comanche nation came to see us. They were a party of about two hundred men, women, and children. We went with them to the south fork of Red River to see their chief, Nicoróco.

We stayed with them a month. We then thought of returning to our old camp, where we had caught our horses, and taking some more; for a great many of those we had captured had died for want of being well cared for. In about five days we arrived at our old camp. The Indians stayed with us but a few days, and then went on in search of buffalo.

When they left, a party of them stole from us eleven head of horses. They were our gentle horses, and all we had for running wild horses; so that we were left unable to do anything. We concluded to pursue the robbers; but this had to be done on foot. Philip Nolan, Robert Ashley, Joseph Reed, David Fero, a negro man called Caesar, and myself, were the volunteers of our small party. We pursued them nine days, and came upon them, encamped on a small creek. They did not see us till we were within fifty yards of them. We went up in a friendly manner.

There were but four men, and some women and children. The rest (twelve men in number) had gone out to kill buffalo. I saw four of our horses close by, feeding. I pointed to them and told the Indians we had come for them, and that they must bring to us the others they had stolen. An old man said the one who had stolen them had taken the others out hunting, but that he would be in that evening. He said the rogue who stole them had but one eye, by which we would know him when he came. They gave us meat, of which they had a large quantity drying; and then we were glad to lie down and rest.

In the evening, as the old man said, One-Eye came up with our horses. We took him and tied him, the others saying nothing, and kept him tied till morning. His wife then gave us all our horses, and we took from the thief all the meat we could conveniently carry. We then told them all that there were but few of us, but we could whip twice their number, and they were of the same opinion. We returned safely to our camp, and found the pen in good repair and all in readiness to run horses.

Discussion

1. What was Nolan's purpose in coming to Texas?
2. Where did he get up his expedition?
3. In what part of Texas did his party find wild horses most plentiful?
4. What game did he find?
5. Where was the Comanche camp?

The Death of Philip Nolan, 1801

In this piece we have accounts of the death of Philip Nolan given by two witnesses, one from each side: Bean, who was in the captured party, and Lieutenant Musquiz, the Spanish officer who captured them. Musquiz's story is taken from his diary.

1 - AS TOLD BY PETER ELLIS BEAN

In four days more it was our misfortune to be attacked attacked by a hundred and fifty Spaniards sent by the commandant at Chihuahua, called Don Salcedo. The troops that came were piloted by Indians from Nacogdoches. They surrounded our camp about one o'clock in the morning, on the 22d of March, 1801. They took the five Spaniards and one American that were guarding our horses, leaving but twelve of us, including Caesar. We were all alarmed by the tramping of their horses; and, as day broke, without speaking a word, they commenced their fire. After about ten minutes our gallant leader, Nolan, was slain by a musket ball which hit him in the head.

In a few minutes they began to fire grape shots at us. They had brought a small swivel on a mule. We had a pen that we had built of logs, to prevent the Indians from stealing from us. From this pen we returned their fire until about nine o'clock. We then had two men wounded and one killed. I told my companions that we ought to charge on the cannon and take it. Two or three agreed to this, but the rest appeared unwilling. I told them it was at most but death; if we stood still all would doubtless be killed; and that we must take the cannon or retreat.

It was agreed that we should retreat. Our number was eleven, of which two were wounded. The powder that we could not put into our horns was given to Caesar to carry, while the rest were to make use of their arms. So we set out through a prairie, and shortly crossed a small creek. While we were defending ourselves, Caesar stopped at the creek and surrendered himself, with the ammunition, to the enemy. Of the two wounded men, one stopped and gave himself up, the other came on with us. There were then nine of us that stood the fire of the enemy, who were on both sides of us, for a march of half a mile. We were so fortunate that not a man of us got hurt, though the balls played around us like hail.

In our march we came to a deep ravine. Here we took refuge and stopped some time. They then began to come too close to us, when we commenced firing afresh. They then retreated. About three o'clock in the afternoon they hoisted a white flag and told us that the commander wanted us to return to our own country and not remain with the Indians. We quickly offered to go with them as companions, but not to give up our arms. It was agreed, and we went back and buried our gallant leader Nolan.

2 - As Told by Lieutenant Musquiz

20th—At daybreak I arrived at the wooden intrenchment. Detained two Indians, who informed me that Nolan and his men were at a place between a creek and some hills, and that they had a house without a roof. As soon as night closed I started, guided by the Tahuaya Indians; and, traveling all night, I arrived before daylight at the place where Nolan was. Concealing our men behind a hill, I waited for the morning.

21st—At sunrise, having divided my force into three bodies—one commanded by me, and carrying a four-pounder—I marched on Nolan's intrenchment. When I was at a distance of about thirty paces from it, ten men sallied from the intrenchment, unarmed.

Among them was Nolan, who said: "Do not approach, because either one or the other will be killed."

Noticing that the men who accompanied Nolan were foreigners, I ordered Mr. William Barr, an Irishman, who had joined my command as interpreter, to speak to them in English, and say that I had come for the purpose of arresting them, and that I expected them to surrender in the name of the king. Nolan had a brief conversation with Barr, and the latter informed me that Nolan and his men were determined to fight.

Nolan immediately entered his intrenchment, followed by his men, and I observed that two Mexicans escaped from the rear of the intrenchment soon after. They joined us, stating that they had brought with them Nolan's carbine, which was handed to me. At daybreak Nolan and his men commenced firing. The fight lasted until nine o'clock a. m, when, Nolan being killed by a cannon ball, his men surrendered. They were out of ammunition. His force at the time of the engagement was composed of fourteen Americans, one Creole of Louisiana, seven Spaniards or Mexicans, and two negro slaves. Nolan had three men wounded and several horses killed. His men had long beards.

After the surrender I learned that they had left Natchez with supplies for two months, and had been in the woods and prairies of Texas over seven months, living on horse meat. Nolan's negroes asked permission to bury their master, which I granted, after causing his ears to be cut off, in order to send them to the governor of Texas.

Discussion

1. Compare the two accounts as to the following points: 81 The day of the fight; who fired first; how early in the fight Nolan fell; what happened after he fell; by what he was killed; the terms of the surrender.

2. Which account do you think is probably the more accurate?

Strike for Liberty
by Bernardo Gutierrez, 1812

After the death of Philip Nolan the ill feeling between the Spaniards and the Americans increased, and the men of our border only waited for a good opportunity to invade Spanish territory. This was found when, in 1811, a revolution broke out in Mexico. Then Augustus Magee, a soldier of the United States, and Bernardo Gutierrez, a Mexican revolutionist, together planned to free Texas from Mexico. In the neutral ground, east of the Sabine River, they raised a force of Mexican and American adventurers. Gutierrez issued this call to the friends of liberty and with a small army conquered east Texas. Then, with a larger force, the leaders together captured La Bahia.

CHIEFS, SOLDIERS, AND CITIZENS: It has been more than a year since I set out from my country (to the United States.) During this time I have worked hard for our good. I had to overcome many difficulties, but I made friends, and found ways for helping us throw off the barbarous and insulting yoke which has oppressed us. Rise all together, soldiers and citizens, and unite in the holy cause of our independence, for on it depends the happiness of our country. Many of our friends have died unjustly under the sword of these tyrants. Their blood from the tomb cries to us for vengeance. Their spirits are before the throne of God praying for our success.

To-day I am marching to your aid with a good sized force of American volunteers, who have left their homes and families to take up our cause and fight for our liberty. These free descendants of men who fought for the independence of the United States know the worth of the liberty their fathers gave to them. And, as our brothers and inhabitants of the same continent, they unsheathe their swords in defense of the cause of humanity, and to drive back the European tyrants to the other side of the Atlantic.

Fellow patriots, your liberty is the object of my efforts. Your rights must be protected and our holy religion must be respected. Awake, awake, rise against the tyrants who try to hold dominion over your lives! The rightful power is in your hands. Use it and you will soon have liberty!

The End of Magee's Expedition
1813

Magee died at La Bahia, but Gutierrez went with the army to San Antonio, captured it, and proclaimed the freedom of Texas. Many of the Americans now went home. Gutierrez's success was short-lived. He was removed from office, and his army, led by Toledo, was soon defeated in a terrible fight at the Medina, which ended the revolution in Texas. The account here given of the battle of the Medina and of the retreat of the insurgents across the province is an "extract of a letter from a gentleman of first respectability" written at Natchitoches, September 4, 1813.

84   I am sorry to inform you that the Republican army was, on the 18th of last month, entirely defeated twenty miles beyond San Antonio by the army of Arredondo.

General Toledo attacked them in their camp with a force of about one to three. The royalists were at first beaten and driven back some distance with the loss of three pieces of cannon and many killed. General Toledo, suspecting an ambuscade, ordered his troops to halt and form on better ground, but the Americans, in spite of the efforts of their officers, rushed into the ambuscade. Many pieces of cannon were opened on them and they were nearly all killed.

Such as were not killed retreated in confusion, leaving everything behind. General Toledo, and Perry, with about sixty others, have arrived at Nacogdoches. Report says there are as many more at the Trinity. W.

B. Wilkinson, who was acting as aid to General Toledo, arrived at Natchitoches yesterday. He returned this morning to enable such as were at Nacogdoches to make a stand and cover the retreating remnant of the army.

Three hundred families left San Antonio and La Bahia for this place, two hundred of them being women on foot. They were escaping the bloody vengeance of Arredondo, who, at Atlimea and Saltillo distinguished himself by putting women and children to death.

It is probable that three hundred Americans are lost, and that the whole country between Rio Grande and the Sabine will be desolated. We can as yet form nothing like a list of the whole number killed. From persons who are hourly arriving here we are led to believe that in a few days we shall have several hundred of the most wretched human beings fleeing from their country and their homes to save their lives. Doctor Forsythe is safe at Nacogdoches. William Slocum, the two Gormleys, and Caston, of the Mississippi territory, are missing.

Discussion

1. Who was Magee? Gutierrez?
2. What was their object in invading Texas?
3. What and where was the Neutral Ground?
4. Of what people was the army composed?
5. On what grounds did Gutierrez appeal to Mexicans? Americans?
6. What was the conduct of the Americans in the battle of the Medina?
7. What do you think of Arredondo?

Some French Filibusters
by Louis Hartmann &
Jean-Baptiste Millard, 1818

In 1818 two French generals, Lallemand and Rigaud, after an attempt to found a colony in Alabama, asked of the Spanish government permission to settle in Texas. This was not granted, but they came, nevertheless, bringing one hundred and twenty colonists. They settled on the Trinity River, about twelve miles above its mouth, and named their abode Champ d'Asile, which means field of refuge. In spite of their high-sounding boast that they would hold by force, if need be, the land on which they were settled, with the first show of hostility on the part of the Spaniards they scurried to Galveston. The pompous language in which Hartmann and Millard, who were in the party, afterward described the enterprise is very amusing when we remember how little they accomplished. Their story, part of which is given here, is really "much ado about nothing."

It seemed that the colony could only continue to prosper. The neighboring Indian tribes felt that they had nothing to fear from our nearness to them, and wished to live on good terms with us. They sent an embassy to offer us the pipe of peace, and to do homage to General Lallemand.

We thought that, being thus at peace with the natives of the country, we should have no cause for fearing the Europeans, who like us, and with no better title to ownership, inhabited the country. How great was our error! We soon learned that the Spanish garrisons of San Antonio and La Bahia, aided by some

86

(the captain) might be found on board the schooner. And to the schooner we accordingly rowed. To our inquiry, Captain Lafitte answered himself, with an invitation to come on board.

My description of this renowned chieftain, to correspond with the original, will shock the preconceived notions of many who have hitherto pictured him as the hero of a novel or a melodrama. I am compelled by truth to introduce him as a stout, rather gentlemanly personage, some five feet ten inches in height, dressed very simply in a foraging cap and blue frock of a most villainous fit. (His complexion, like most creoles, was olive; his countenance full, mild, and rather impressive but for a small black eye which now and then, as he grew animated in conversation, would flash in a way which impressed me with a notion that "El Capitan" might be, when roused, a very "ugly customer."

His demeanor toward us was exceedingly courteous, and upon learning Captain Kearny's mission, he invited us below, and tendered "the hospitalities of the vessel."

"I am making my arrangements," Lafitte observed, "to leave the bay. The ballast of the brig has been shifted. As soon as we can get her over the bar we sail."

"We supposed that your flotilla was larger," Captain Kearny remarked.

"I have men on shore," said Lafitte—not apparently noticing the remark—"who are destroying the fort, and preparing some spars for the brig. Will you go on shore and look at what I am doing?"

We returned to the deck, and Lafitte pointed us to the preparations which had been made on board the brig for getting her to sea. The schooner on which we were, mounted a long gun amidships and six nine pounders a side. There were, I should think, fifteen or twenty men on deck, apparently of all nations; and below I could see there were a great many more.

There was no appearance of any uniform among them, nor, to the eyes of a man-of-war's man, much discipline. The officers, or those who appeared such, were in plain clothes, and Lafitte himself was without any distinguishing mark of his rank.

On the shore we passed a long shed under which a party was at work, and around which junk, cordage, sails, and all sorts of heterogeneous matters were scattered in confusion. Beyond this we came across a four-gun fort. It had been advantageously located, and was a substantial looking affair, but now was nearly dismantled, and a gang was completing the work of destruction.

"You see, Captain, I am getting ready to leave. I am friendly to your country. Ah, they call me a pirate. But I am not a pirate. You see there?" said he, pointing suddenly toward the point of the beach.

"I see," said our skipper, "what does that mean?"

The object to which our attention was thus directed was the dead body of a man dangling from a rude gibbet erected on the beach.

"That is my justice. That vaurien (good-for-nothing) plundered an American schooner. The captain complained to me of him, and he was found guilty and hung. Will you go on board my brig?"

On this vessel there was evidently a greater attention paid to discipline. Lafitte led the way into his cabin, where preparation had already been made for dinner, to partake of which we were invited. Sea air and exercise are proverbial persuaders of the appetite; and Mr. Lafitte's display of good stew, dried fish, and wild turkey was more tempting than prize money.

Under the influence of the most generous and racy wines he became quite sociable. Lafitte was evidently educated and gifted with no common talent for conversation.

"I should like very much to hear your life, Captain," I remarked.

He smiled and shrugged his shoulders. "It is nothing extraordinary," he said. "I can tell it in a very few words. But there was a time"—and he drew a long breath—"when I could not tell it without cocking both pistols."

"Eighteen years ago I was a merchant in San Domingo. My father before me was a merchant. I had become rich. I had married me a wife. I determined to go to Europe, and I wound up all my affairs in the West Indies. I sold my property there. I bought a ship and loaded her, besides which, I had on board a large amount of specie—all that I was worth, in short. Well, sir, when the vessel that I was on had been a week at sea we were overhauled by a Spanish man-of-war. The Spaniards captured us. They took everything—goods, specie, even my wife's jewels. They set us on shore on a barren sand key, with just provisions enough to keep us alive a few days. An American schooner took us off, and landed us in New Orleans. I did not care

91

what became of me. I was a beggar. My wife took the fever from exposure and hardship, and died in three days after my arrival. I met some daring fellows who were as poor as I was. We bought a schooner, and declared against Spain eternal war. Fifteen years I have carried on a war against Spain. So long as I live I am at war with Spain, but no other nation. I am at peace with the world, except Spain. Although they call me a pirate, I am not guilty of attacking any vessel of the English or French. I showed you the place where my own people have been punished for plundering American property."

Discussion

1. Who was Lafitte?
2. Where were his headquarters?
3. What did he say was his reason for becoming a pirate?
4. How did the government of the United States regard him?
5. Did he leave Galveston Island when he promised to? (Study the introduction.)

The Last of the Filibusters
by Mirabeau B. Lamar, 1819

Between 1803 and 1819 Texas was claimed by both the United States and Spain. In 1819, after the United States had given up her claim, Dr. James Long organized an expedition in Natchez, Mississippi, and went to Texas for the purpose of taking it from Spain and establishing an independent republic. This selection describes the failure of his first expedition. General Lamar got his information for this account from Mrs. Long.

Long was by nature a soldier, and had always sighed after a proper field for the indulgence of his military spirit. The citizens of Natchez resolved to make one more effort in behalf of the liberties of that oppressed and bleeding province (Texas.) A meeting was accordingly held by the inhabitants, and arrangements entered into for an immediate and vigorous assault upon the country. The command was tendered to General Long. He accepted the responsibility with pride and pleasure, and entered at once upon the duties of the station.

His activity and zeal soon rendered the project quite popular. He pledged the whole of his private fortune in the enterprise. With the best wishes for his welfare, he left Natchez with about seventy-five of the most hardy and intrepid followers, on the 17th of June, 1819. As he pushed from the shore, a shot from the cannon was fired to his success. He pushed for Natchitoches, where he had means of his own, and many friends; thence to the Sabine, and on to Nacogdoches. Here, in a short time after his arrival, he was able to muster about three hundred strong.

Long's designs were by many either misunderstood or misrepresented. The expedition was to get possession of the country, to rescue it from the grasp of tyranny, and secure its settlement by North Americans.

General Long hoped to achieve by military operations what the two Austins had the ability and address to accomplish by peaceful negotiations.

At Nacogdoches the council met on the 22d of June, 1819, and on the succeeding day declared the province a free and independent republic.

General Long then made preparation to go to Galveston, for the purpose of establishing a small post at Bolivar Point, and also to obtain, if possible, some munitions of war from the celebrated lord of that island, Jean Lafitte. He had already opened a correspondence with this bold rover of the seas. Persuaded that some assistance might be obtained from the pirate by a personal interview, the general resolved upon a visit.

At this time his wife arrived. Leaving her in the family of a Mr. Amberson, he departed for the island, taking with him thirteen men. And now commenced the calamities of the whole expedition. On arriving at the Coshattie (Indian) village, the very first thing that saluted his ears was the unexpected tidings of the enemy's approach. The Indians reported the Spaniards as advancing rapidly, seven hundred strong.

Orders were immediately dispatched to Cook, Walker, and David Long, to repair forthwith to this village, where he intended to give the invaders battle.

He hastened with all possible speed to Galveston Island, but, not receiving the expected assistance, returned without delay to the village. Here he was greeted by a letter from his wife, dated a day or two after his departure from Nacogdoches, apprising him of the approach of the enemy, and of the disorganized condition of that post.

Exasperated at the conduct of Cook, he mounted his horse and dashed for Nacogdoches. On the way he met his wife, hurrying from the place.

The town was now entirely deserted, with no human being in it except himself. He commenced gathering the public arms and ammunition, and while he was busily concealing them in an old dry well, he heard his name whispered. The man who called him was so worn down by hunger and fatigue that Long did not recognize his faithful lieutenant.

"My name," said the wretched being, "is Lightle."

At the mention of Lightle, Long rushed to his support. This brave and suffering lieutenant was attached to Johnson's party, and from him Long now received an account of the fate of that unfortunate company. They had been surprised and defeated.

"And what of Walker and my brother David?" inquired the general.

"Of them," said Lightle, "I know nothing."

This news fell heavy on the heart of Long; he read in it the ruin of his expedition. After taking his wife to Natchitoches, General Long himself returned to Texas. At Bolivar Point he collected the scattered fragments of his ruined forces, and learned from them the sorrowful tidings of their sufferings.

Discussion

1. What was the object of Long's expedition?
2. How large was his force?
3. Why did he think that Lafitte might help him?
4. Write a short sketch of the failure of the expedition.

A Battle with the Cannibals
by James Long, 1819

This account of a battle with the Karankawa Indians is taken from a letter which General Long wrote in August, 1819, to a friend in New Orleans.

On the 30th of August I surprised and gave battle to the Carankawa Indians. They are a race of cannibals who have within a few years murdered and eaten more than two hundred Americans.

We had every advantage in point of attack, as they felt in perfect security until we were within forty yards, charging on them.

They were fully four to one, and the battle lasted fifteen minutes. Their loss was terrible; ours one killed and nine severely wounded. Two have since died, the others are still dangerous.

A few women and children were unavoidably killed in the action. These Indians fight with bows and arrows, spears and tomahawks.

I am building a strong fort on a beautiful peninsula between the Gulf of Mexico and Trinity Bay.

How General Long Won His Bride
by Mirabeau B. Lamar, 1815

After Stephen F. Austin began the settlement of Texas, Mrs. Long came to his colony. During the period of the revolution she lived at Brazoria, and it was through conversations with her that General Lamar heard this story.

In the spring of 1815, there dwelt near the city of Natchez, a young belle of great loveliness, whose wit and beauty were increased by the refinement of her manners and the purity of her sentiments. Attracting the attention of all, she was wooed unwon by suitors of the highest renown. She was now arrived at the age when the laws of Mississippi require an orphan child to choose a guardian. Accident led to the choice which she made. Whether it was a prudent and judicious one, the reader must determine when he hears the sequel.

Tying a sunbonnet of green silk under her fair round chin, and slinging her satchel on her arm, she was about to obey the summons of the academy bell, when she was suddenly stopped by a little negro girl, who announced that a stranger had just gone into the sick man's room.

"And what is that to me?" said the youthful beauty. "Do his friends not call upon him every day?"

"But this is the handsomest man in the world," replied the servant, "and I want you to see him before you go to school."

Now, the handsomest man in the world was certainly a sight worth seeing. Accordingly, she doffed her bonnet and threw aside her books, with a determination to take a peep at this fair Adonis. Whether she stole a glance at the mirror to adjust her shining ringlets, is a matter of which fame reported not; but it is said that she never looked more lovely in her life than when the visitor entered the parlor.

His personal appearance came up fully to her expectations; and although he was not the handsomest man in the world, he nevertheless possessed a very commanding figure—tall, active and erect, with a fiery eye and a martial tread, the very hero for a tale of love and war. His name and the purpose of his visit were mysteries soon explained. He was a surgeon in the army, and had come to prescribe for one of his companions in arms.

In a few minutes the happy couple, mutually pleased, found themselves seated by the window, contending with each other in a game of draughts. The lady of course was victor, and won of her antagonist a pair of gloves. The payment of this debt formed a fair pretext for our hero to renew his visit on the succeeding day.

"I come," said he, "to settle accounts, for debts of honor must be punctually paid." The lady, however, declined receiving the gloves on the ground that she played for amusement only.

"Then," said the gentleman, "if you will not take them as your due, you must accept them as a present."

To this the lady could not politely demur, and as she put forth her snowy fingers to receive the gloves, the happy donor, in a tone between jocularity and earnest, expressed a wish that the hand that gave might go with the gift. This was enough. The lady understood the hint, and was pleased to see how the wind was blowing. In a short time they were open and avowed lovers.

But it is known that the course of true love never did run smooth. The friends of the lady objected to the union on the very good grounds of the youth and in experience of the parties, and for a good while the opposition seemed in a fair way to defeat the wishes of the sighing couple. Chance and courage, however, decided the matter.

We have already told that our young heroine would shortly have to choose her guardian. The time for making this selection was now arrived; and being called upon to name her choice, she turned and pointed to her lover. Her friends remonstrated; she was obstinate. They scolded; she persisted. At length, when it became obvious that she really intended what she said, all further hostility ceased, and it was not many days before the delighted lover was hailed in the family in the double capacity of guardian and husband.

They were married on the fourteenth of May, eighteen hundred and fifteen, the bride being in her fourteenth year, and the bridegroom in his twentieth.

And ask ye who were the parties? The lady's maiden name was Jane H. Wilkinson, the niece of General Wilkinson. She was born in Charles County, Maryland, and losing her father at an early age, removed with her mother to the State of Mississippi in eighteen hundred and eleven. The hero of the story is no other than the chivalrous General Long.

99

Discussion
1. What was Mrs. Long's name before her marriage?
2. Where did General Long first meet her?
3. How did she defeat the opponents of her marriage?

Mrs. Long's Adventures in Texas
by Mirabeau B. Lamar, 1819

The history of Mrs. Long is so intimately connected with that of her husband, and is of itself so full of interest, that it cannot be omitted. A few days after his departure she resolved to follow her husband and share his destiny, in spite of her feeble condition and the entreaties of her friends. He was in a foreign country; in the midst of peril, with no home but the camp and a no safety but his sword. To attempt such a journey, through a wilderness of savages in a distant land, with her two little children and no human assistance except a small negro girl, displays a resolution and fortitude which nothing but the tenderest feelings of the human heart could inspire.

She started on the 28th of June. Mr. James Rowan, the friend of her husband and a wealthy merchant of the place, hearing that she was about to embark, came to the river bank to see her off and bid her farewell. He found her in tears. And well might she weep. She was not only leaving the home of her happier days, but she was going, she knew not where, on a long journey in a strange land, with ruined health, almost destitute of means, and without a friendly hand to aid her on her way. These things pressed upon the heart, but the burden was quickly lightened by the generous Rowan.

Unprepared as he was for such a trip, he nevertheless stepped into the boat, and offered to see her on her journey as far as her sister Calvert's, in Alexandria. In a few minutes they were gliding down the river.

The journey to Alexandria was protracted and distressing. The weather was bad, accommodations worse; and the boat finally stopping on the route, a messenger had to be dispatched to Alexandria for means of conveyance. After much delay, a courier made his appearance with a couple of horses. Mrs. Long and her servant girl mounted one of the animals, and Mr. Rowan the other, with the little daughter Ann behind him and the infant in his arms. They completed the balance of the route, exhausted with fatigue and drenched with rain.

For more than four weeks Mrs. Long remained at her sister's dangerously ill. The physicians advised her to prosecute her journey without delay, which she could do, they said, by making short stages and avoiding exposure. She accordingly set out in a closed carriage, leaving her infant to the care of Mrs. Calvert.

Tarrying a few days at Natchitoches, she proceeded to the Sabine, where she expected to be met by her husband. He had been there the day previous according to appointment, but could not wait her arrival. At Mr. Gaines's she remained a couple of days to regain her strength, and then resumed her journey. She reached Nacogdoches and experienced in the warm welcome of her husband an ample compensation for all her toils and sufferings past. She arrived upon the very eve of calamity. A few weeks only, of perpetual excitement and alarm, were spent with her husband, prior to his leaving for Galveston. He had scarcely turned his back, however, when he received tidings of the enemy's approach.

Writing his wife to retire to a Mr. Brown's as a place of safety, he hastened to Galveston Island. Not receiving the desired and expected assistance from that quarter, he returned without delay. On the way he met his wife flying from Nacogdoches. She told him that it was useless to proceed; that all was lost. This only made him the more restless. Leaving his lady in Mr. Brown's family, he put the rowels to his horse, and after riding all night, reached Nacogdoches. The town was now entirely deserted, with no human being in it except himself. On arriving again at Mr. Brown's, where he had left his lady and still expected to join her, he found the family had fled.

The whole population were rushing like a terrified herd of buffalo to the Sabine. The enemy, who had entered Nacogdoches in an hour after Long left it, were rushing in pursuit of the flying people. Fortunately for Mrs. Long she had followed the upper road. Her husband took the same, and after traveling all night reached the river as the sun was rising. The day was spent in crossing the stream.

That night Mrs. Long received information of the death of her infant. Taking an affectionate leave of her husband at Natchitoches, she proceeded to her sister Calvert's, where she arrived some time in the early part of November, a little upwards of four months from the date of her departure from Natchez.

Discussion

1. Describe the hardships of Mrs. Long's journey to Texas.
2. Write a brief account of her experience in Texas.
3. Compare this piece with previous ones about the Longs. What new facts does this one tell about General Long's disasters?

PART THREE
Anglo-American Colonization

Come Out to the West

Anonymous verse, widely printed
in eastern newspapers in the 1840s.

Come forth from your cities,
Come out to the West;
Ye have hearts, ye have hands,
Leave to nature the rest:
The prairie, the forest,
The stream at command—
"The world is too crowded?"
Pshaw! come and take land.

Come, travel the mountain
And paddle the stream;
The cabin shall smile and
The corn patch shall gleam:
"A wife and six children!"
'Tis wealth in your hand;
Your axe and your rifle—
Out West and take land.

Difficulties of an Empresario
by Stephen F. Austin, 1823

The following extract is from a letter written by Austin in 1823 to an official of the government of Mexico.

MOST EXCELLENT SIR:

In the month of December, 1821, I removed the first families and commenced the settlement, and then hastened to Bexar to receive the further instructions of the government. On my arrival at that place, I was advised by the governor and my other friends to proceed direct to Mexico, and receive authority to make titles to the settlers for their lands. I accordingly departed for Mexico, and arrived in that city in April, 1822.

On my arrival in (return to) the colony, which I had commenced nearly two years before, I found that most of the colonists, discouraged by my long absence and the uncertainty in which they had been for such a length of time, had returned to the United States, and that the few who remained, hard pressed and harassed on every side by hostile Indians, and threatened with the horrors of famine, in consequence of the drought, were on the eve of breaking up and leaving the province. Encouraged, however, by my return, we persevered through the complicated and appalling difficulties which surrounded us, until the new crops yielded us bread.

Since my arrival I have been most industriously laboring (in conjunction with the Baron de Bastrop) in completing the affairs of the colony, and I hope to make a finish of them in a few months more, though, owing to the many unfavorable reports propagated by those who returned, and my delay in Mexico, many of the families who at first intended to come have not done so. This has produced some delay in completing the three hundred families which I am permitted to settle in this colony.

The situation I am placed in (near the frontiers of two nations, surrounded on every side by hostile Indians, and exposed to their attacks, and to the no less vexatious pilferings and robbings of those tribes who profess friendship, but steal whenever an occasion presents) renders my task peculiarly laborious and difficult, and requires a most severe and efficient police to keep out and punish fugitives and vagabonds from both nations. I have experienced some difficulty on this subject, owing to the want of a more full and ample authority relative to the punishment of crimes. The most excellent deputation of Monterey ordered me by their decree to condemn criminals to hard labor on public works, until the superior government should decide their case, and to punish them in no other way. But a difficulty arises in executing this order.

We are forty to fifty leagues from Bexar and have no jail, no troops to guard prisoners; and a condemnation to hard labor, without an adequate guard to enforce the decree, is only to exasperate a criminal, make him laugh at the laws and the civil authorities, and turn him loose on society to commit new depredations. I have, therefore, in some cases been driven to the painful alternative of either permitting a criminal to escape unpunished, or of taking upon myself the responsibility of inflicting corporal punishment.

If these difficulties could be remedied by vesting authority in some tribunal here to punish crimes by corporal punishment, and—in case of foreigners—banishment from the province, I think it would greatly tend to the good order of this part of the province.

I have made it a rule not to admit any settler who does not produce the most unequivocal evidence of good moral character and industrious habits, and I will vouch for those received by me, that they will not form undutiful nor ungrateful citizens and subjects of the nation that has so kindly received them.

I hope Your Excellency will pardon me for troubling you with so long a letter, but as I before observed, the future fate of myself and followers must depend upon the good opinion and protection which the government of our adoption may be pleased to extend to us.

Discussion

1. What was the object of Austin's visit to Mexico?
2. What changes took place in the colony during his absence?
3. Who assisted Austin in founding the colony?
4. In what ways did the Indians annoy the settlers?
5. What difficulties did Austin meet in executing the laws?
6. What precautions did he take to secure good colonists?

Punishing Indian Horse Thieves
by J. H. Kuykendall, 1823

Mr. Kuykendall wrote this in 1856. His father was one of the earliest settlers of Texas.

Towards the latter part of this summer (1823) a party of Tonkawas stole a horse from father and several from Mr. Wheat. Father, Thomas Boatright, my brother Barzillai, and myself pursued the thieves. For a few miles the trail went northward; it then turned southward or down the country. Suspecting the Tonkawas, and learning that a portion of the tribe under the chief Carita were somewhere near "the Fort" (Fort Bend) on the Brazos, we resolved to proceed to that point. When we arrived at the fort we learned that the Tonkawas were encamped on Big Creek six or eight miles below that place.

We immediately returned to the infant town of San Felipe—then containing but two or three log cabins—and reported our suspicions of the Tonkawas. Austin raised a few men and went with us to the fort, where we were joined by a few more men, making our force thirty strong. (Austin dispatched two men to look for the Tonkawas, but before they returned Carita came to us and acknowledged that five of his young men had stolen our horses. He said the horses should be restored and the thieves punished. We immediately proceeded to the camp of the Indians, where all the horses were promptly restored, save one, which Carita promised to deliver next day.

He pointed out the five men who had committed the theft. Each of them was sentenced to receive fifty lashes and have one-half of his head shaved. Carita inflicted one-half of the stripes and my father the other half. The lash was very lightly laid on by Carita, who frequently paused to ask Austin "cuantos?" (Spanish for how many.) Before he had inflicted his half of the stripes the culprits pretended to swoon; but as soon as father began to apply the hair. lash they were roused to the most energetic action.

The sentence was fully executed on four of the thieves. The remaining one, being sick, was excused from the whipping, but was to have his head polled after his brother offenders were disposed of; but while the castigation was proceeding, the sick man managed to save his locks by running off and concealing himself in a thicket. We returned to the fort, and next day Carita delivered us the missing horse.

Discussion

1. What tribe of Indians troubled the settlers?
2. Describe the way the party was organized to pursue the thieves.
3. What punishment was given the culprits?
4. How was it administered?

How a Colonist Came to Texas
by Noah Smithwick, 1827

*This selection describes some of the inconveniences and hard-
ships of travel experienced by the pioneers of Texas in coming
here.*

PART ONE

What the discovery of gold was to California the
colonization act of 1825 was to Texas. In the following
year Sterling C. Robertson, who had obtained a grant
for a colony, for each 100 families of which he was to
receive a bonus of 23,025 acres of land, went up into
Kentucky recruiting. The glowing terms in which he
talked of the advantages to be gained by emigration
were well calculated to further his scheme.

To every head of a family, if a farmer, was promised
177 acres of farming land and 4,428 acres of pasture
land for stock; colonists to be exempt from taxation
six years from date of settlement, with the privilege
of importing, duty free, everything they might desire
for themselves and families; an abundance of game,
wild horses, cattle, turkeys, buffalo, deer and antelope
by the drove. The woods abounded in bee trees, wild
grapes, plums, cherries, persimmons, haws and dew-
berries, while walnuts, hickory nuts and pecans were
abundant along the water courses.

The climate was so mild that houses were not essential; neither was an abundance of clothing or bedding—buffalo robes and bear skins supplying all that
was needed for the latter and buckskin the former.

Corn in any quantity was to be had for the planting, and, in short, there the primitive curse was set at defiance. Mexican soldiers were stationed on the frontier to keep the Indians in check.

Of the hardships and privations, the ever increasing danger from the growing dissatisfaction of the Indians, upon whose hunting grounds the whites were steadily encroaching, and the almost certainty of an ultimate war with Mexico, he was discreetly silent. Viewed from that distance, the prospect was certainly flattering, and it should not occasion surprise that men with large families were induced to migrate thither with the hope of securing homes for themselves and children.

I was but a boy in my nineteenth year, and in for Texas adventure. My older brothers talked of going. They abandoned the project; but it had taken complete possession of me. So, early in the following year, 1827, I started out from Hopkinsville, Kentucky, with all my worldly possessions, which consisted of a few dollars in money, a change of clothes, and a gun, of course, to seek my fortune in this lazy man's paradise.

Part Two

Incredible as it may seem to the present generation, seeing the country traversed from ocean to ocean, and from lakes to gulf with innumerable lines of railroad, there was not then a mile of railroad in operation in the United States; and though twenty years had elapsed since the *Clermont* made her triumphal trip from New York to Albany, few steamboats plied the western waters and none had ventured out to sea.

The stagecoach, the only public overland conveyance, took me down to the mouth of the river, where
I intended to take steamer for New Orleans; but the
steamboat had not arrived and no one knew when
it would. My impatience could not brook delay, so I
took passage on a flatboat, or as they were known in
river parlance, a "Mississippi broadhorn," the poor
man's transfer."

Out on the broad bosom of the Father of Waters
these boats floated from the Ohio, the Cumberland,
the Tennessee, laden with the products of the vast region adjoining, to be floated down to New Orleans
and thence distributed around the seaboard by sailing vessels. The flatboat, after serving its purpose,
was broken up and sold for lumber and fuel, while the
owner pocketed his cash and wended his way home,
generally on foot up through Mississippi, where he
was liable to be interviewed by footpads and relieved
of his money if not of his life. Many were the horrible
stories of robbery and murder thus committed by old
John A. Murril and his band of freebooters.

My transport was loaded with ice, artificial ice being a thing then unheard of. The crew consisted of
three men, whose principal duty was to look out for
sunken trees, and to keep clear of eddies, for a boat
once drawn into the swirl would go floating around,
in danger of colliding with the drift and being sunk.
As flatboats never returned and seldom passed each
other, the slow, leisurely drifting, day the poor saw-
yers, after day, became intolerably monotonous. So
I stopped off at Natchez and waited for a steamboat.
Very poetical it was, no doubt, this dropping down

with the rippling stream, but I had not started out in search of the poetical.

By the time I reached New Orleans my money was running low and mechanics were getting big wages, so I went to work in the old Leeds foundry.

When the sickly season came on and the men began to leave, I again took up the line of march for Texas, this time on board a coasting schooner, laden with supplies for the Mexican army. A steam tug towed us out to the mouth of the Mississippi as far as steamers ventured. The weather was lovely as a dream of Venice, and we sped away on the wings of the tradewinds. We passed Galveston Island in plain view. There was no sign of human habitation on it; nothing to give promise of the thriving city which now covers it. It was only noted then as having been the headquarters of Lafitte and his pirates, and as such was pointed out to me. The trip was a delightful one, and I was in fine spirits. On the third day we threaded the Paso Caballo and ran into Matagorda Bay, having made the run in a little over forty-eight hours, a remarkable record in those days.

We cast anchor in the mouth of the Lavaca River, where we had calculated to find the Mexican troops; but there were no troops, no agent, no one authorized to receive the goods. There was not an American there. The colonization law exempted from settlement all land within twenty-five miles of the coast, so the territory was given over to the Karankawa Indians, a fierce tribe, whose hand was against every man. A few Mexicans came around, but they spoke no English and I understood no Spanish.

At length two men, Fulcher and McHenry, who had squatted on land six or eight miles up the river, sighted the schooner and came down in a dugout. They took me in with them and I spent my first night in Texas in their cabin. My first meal on Texas soil was dried venison sopped in honey. Next morning I set out on foot for De Witt's colony, ten miles further up on the Lavaca.

Discussion

1. Name the different inducements that led Mr. Smithwick to come to Texas.

2. Describe the seven different means of travel that he employed in his journey.

3. To what country did Texas belong in 1827?

4. Where was De Witt's colony located?

The First Sunday School in Texas
by Thomas J. Pilgrim, 1829

This selection shows the condition of schools as well as of Sunday schools in the pioneer settlements.

In the fall of 1828, I started from the western part of the State of New York for Texas. I was in company with sixty others, men, women, and children, under the leadership of Elias R. Wightman. He had resided about three years in the country, and his intelligence, energy, and enterprise well fitted him to be the leader of a colony.

I soon engaged in teaching, and succeeded in a short time in raising a school of about forty scholars, mostly boys. I felt the necessity of moral and religious, as well as intellectual culture, and resolved to make an effort to found a Sunday school. Notice was given through the school that on the following Sunday an address would be delivered on the subject.

I was gratified to see at the time appointed a large and respectful audience assembled. An address was delivered. They seemed to feel interested, and on the following Sunday a school was organized of thirty-two scholars. There were not lacking intelligent gentlemen and ladies to act as teachers, but of the other appurtenances of a well regulated Sunday school we had none. This lack was supplied as best it could be by contributions from the citizens of such books as they had, and by the oral instructions of superintendent and teachers.

The next Sunday found the school underway, and giving promise of great success. A lecture was delivered each Sunday morning, intended for both old and

115

young, and to hear these lectures people came from the distance of ten miles.

Now let us for a moment contemplate this little Sunday school. In a blackjack and post oak grove near the center of the town is a rude log cabin about eighteen by twenty-two feet, the roof covered with boards held down by weight poles, the logs unhewn, and the cracks neither chinked nor battened, and a dirt floor. Across it are placed several logs hewn on one side for seats. At one end stands the superintendent, a mere stripling. Before him are about half a dozen gentlemen and ladies as teachers, and thirty two children, without any of those appendages which are now considered necessary to a well conducted Sunday school.

I would here correct an erroneous impression in relation to the character of the early settlers of Texas. A kinder and more hospitable people perhaps never lived. Their houses were welcome homes to each other; and never was the stranger rudely repulsed or sent empty away.

New Englanders have always been proud of their Christian ancestors who bequeathed to them so rich an inheritance. Well may the present generation of Texans look back with gratitude and pride to those noble souled heroes who by their toils, energy, self sacrifice, and daring, won and bequeathed to them the fairest land on which the sun ever shone.

Discussion

1. How was the first Sunday school started in Texas?
2. Describe the building and its furniture.
3. Compare it with the Sunday school that you attend.
4. What do we owe to the early settlers of Texas?
5. Did all of the colonists come from the southern States?

A Disappointed Land Speculator
Writer Unknown, 1831

Early in the month of March, 1831, I reached New Orleans on my way from the northern States to Texas. My principal object was to examine the condition of the large tract of land I had purchased of the Galveston Bay and Texas Land Company. There was a vessel at that time preparing to sail for Brazoria, a place on the river Brazos; and I took passage on board. After stipulating for the price of twenty dollars and providing myself with a few conveniences for the voyage, I embarked with fifty-three other passengers, of different descriptions and colors.

Before leaving New Orleans I had sought in vain for any satisfactory information concerning the country to which I was bound; and was but little more fortunate in my inquiries among the passengers, most of whom were going to live in Texas. Among these were an old Tennessean and his wife, with their sons, two young men, who were going "to hunt land." There was also a man from Alabama, who had some negroes with him, going to take up his abode in Texas; but he had nothing to communicate concerning the country, except some very favorable general accounts he had received from his friends. On reaching

117

New Orleans he had learned for the first time that slaves cannot be held in the Mexican territory, and had taken measures which had been recommended to him to evade the general law of abolition. He had obtained their attested signatures to articles of indenture, by which they had bound themselves to him for ninety-nine years. He counseled another man who was on board with his wife and several slaves, to do the same, and gave them such instructions as were necessary to render the pretended agreement binding on the negroes.

The scenes around me afforded certainly a noble view, even for a spectator personally uninterested in the soil; but to the proprietor of a vast tract of land, like myself, a finer could hardly be imagined. I had doubtless made a judicious purchase, and in what a country! How nobly would twenty thousand acres look, wherever I might determine to locate my estate! Twenty thousand acres! Twenty thousand acres! What an estate! How many cattle and human inhabitants would it be able to support.

I had some agreeable reflections to make as I passed up the Brazos. I expected, on my arrival at Brazoria, to obtain all information necessary to guide me to some of the company's land, to apply to the company's surveyor to locate me twenty thousand acres wherever I should direct him, and to secure a clear title from the company's agents. I had been given to understand that surveyors and agents would be found on the spot, ready to act and able to perform all the stipulations which I had been led to suppose they had bound themselves to.

At Brazoria I had some conversation with Mr. William Austin on the purchase of land I had made in New York, but the result was not such as to afford me much gratification. On the contrary, he regarded the certificate I held as of no value whatever. He was confident that the government would never recognize the right, claimed by the company, of giving titles to lands; for, as he said, it had not even been conferred upon the empresarios, from whom the company pretended to have received it. He had already seen several persons who had come out under circumstances like my own, and who, on inquiry, had become convinced that they could effect nothing. I soon learned that my worst fears were too well founded, and that my hopes were all fallacious.

I had now some painful and mortifying reflections to make. On an examination of the subject with the facts before me, I found that I derived no advantage whatever from the payment of money I had made, having not a foot of land, nor any claim to offer superior to that of any man who might come to Texas from a foreign country. My confidence in the names of a few respectable individuals appended to the advertisements of a company had betrayed me into much disappointment, as well as some pecuniary loss.

When I ascertained the facts in the case, I could not think of myself alone. I knew that numbers had already come out to Texas under impressions as erroneous as my own, and supposed that many more were on the way. I believed, too, that the company were still selling scrip, and that probably hundreds of persons, families and all, had by this time embarked in the same incautious speculation.

Discussion

1. What was the writer's purpose in coming to Texas?
2. By what route did he come?
3. Compare the cost of transportation then and to-day.
4. Note the lack of knowledge of Texas shown by the passengers.
5. How was the Mexican law concerning slaves evaded?
6. What were the writer's reflections as he passed up the Brazos?
7. Describe his disappointment.
8. Was he the only immigrant who was thus disappointed?

Breaking Mustangs
Writer Unknown, 1831

My two new friends intended to proceed immediately to Anahuac; and I concluded to accompany them, as that would be the most probable point for the early reception of news, from the United States, several vessels with emigrants being understood to be on the passage.

The first thing to be attended to was the purchase of a horse; and this was readily done. The small horses of the country, called mustangs, introduced by the Spaniards, and now numerous in the more northern prairies, run wild in droves over these parts of Texas, and are easily taken and rendered serviceable by the inhabitants. When caught, it would be a problem to a stranger to confine them, where there is neither tree nor rock to be found; but the Mexicans put on a halter, knot it at the end, dig a hole about ten inches deep, put in the knot, and press the earth down upon it. The pull being sidewise is at a disadvantage, and the horse is unable to draw it out. They are driven to market, purchased for three or four dollars, branded, hobbled, turned out again, and entirely abandoned to themselves until they are needed.

Whenever a vessel arrives, some of the inhabitants send into the woods and cane brakes for such a number as they suppose may be wanted by the passengers; and this I found had already been done, in anticipation of the wants of those who came in the sloop

121

Majesty. In the log stable belonging to Mr. Austin, at whose house I lodged, I saw a number of them, with all the wild look which might be expected from their habits of life. They are small, generally about thirteen hands high, well formed, rather for strength, and of different colors. I saw others in several other stables; and at length made choice of a white one. Having paid for him a doubloon and four dollars (a handsome advance on his original cost), I stuffed a pair of saddle bags with a few articles of food as well as clothes, and was soon ready for my journey.

As the brands on horses afford the only evidence of their identity, and the property of their owners, the rules observed in respect to them are very strict. These horses are very useful in the country, and may perhaps become at some future time a valuable article of export, as they are innumerable, and cost only the trouble of catching. This is done with a strong noosed cord, made of twisted strips of raw hide, and called a lazo, which is the Spanish word for band or bond. It has been often described, as well as the manner of throwing it, as it is in common use for catching animals, and sometimes for choking men, in different parts of America inhabited by the descendants of the Spanish and Portuguese.

A man on horseback, with a lazo coiled in his left hand, and one end of it fastened to the horse, whirls the noosed end in the air over his head as he approaches the animal he intends to seize; and, on finding an opportunity, throws it over its head or horns, and checks his horse. The noose is instantly drawn tight, and the poor creature is thrown violently down, without the power of moving, and generally deprived of breath. They are sometimes badly injured, and even killed, by being dashed to the ground, but generally escape with a severe practical lesson on the nature of this rude instrument of civilization, which they afterwards hold in great respect all their lives, yielding immediately whenever they feel it again upon their neck.

The mustangs often carry to their graves evidence of the violent means adopted by the Mexicans in breaking them to the bridle. Many of them are foundered or otherwise diseased. A horse which has been lazoed is blindfolded, and, after having their terrible lever bits put into his mouth, a moderate pull upon which might break his jaw, is mounted by a rider armed with the heavy and barbarous spurs of the country. If he runs he is pricked to his speed till he falls down with exhaustion. He is then turned in the opposite direction and cruelly spurred again. If he is able to run back to the point from which he started, he is thought to have bottom enough to make a valuable horse, otherwise he is turned off as good for little or nothing. The process is a brutal one, and the agony inflicted by the bits is extreme. The blood flows freely from the mouth which is often greatly swollen, and the animal yields to mere force.

The white hunters have another method of taking the wild horses which is often successful. It is called creasing, and is done by shooting them with a rifle ball upon a particular cord or tendon in the neck, immediately under the mane. If the ball takes effect precisely in the right spot the animal falls benumbed,

123

and without the power to move for several minutes, when he is easily secured. Should it strike too low, the horse is still able to run off, but eventually dies.

Discussion

1. Do you know whether there were any horses in America when Columbus discovered the continent?
2. What do you suppose was the origin of the wild horses in Texas?
3. In what ways did the Texans catch mustangs?
4. Describe the cruel method of breaking them.
5. Describe an old Mexican bit.
6. What was the ordinary price of a mustang?
7. Besides using them as work animals, what other use was sometimes made of them by the early settlers?

Among the Old Three Hundred
by Noah Smithwick

Stephen F. Austin's first permit from the government of Mexico to found a colony in Texas provided that he should settle three hundred families. For this reason, those who settled in his first colony were called "The Old Three Hundred."

They were a social people, those old Three Hundred, though no one seems to have noted the evidence of it. There were a number of weddings and other social gatherings during my sojourn in that section. The most notable one, perhaps, was the marriage of Nicholas McNutt to Miss Cartwright. Both the families occupied prominent social positions, and there was a large number of invited guests. Jesse Cartwright, father of the bride, was a man in comfortable circumstances, and he and his family were people of good breeding. They were among the very first of Austin's colonists. The bridegroom was a son of the widow McNutt, also among the early arrivals. Miss Mary Allen, daughter of Martin Allen, a very pretty girl and a great belle, by the way, was bridesmaid. John McNutt, brother of the bridegroom, was groomsman.

There being no priest in the vicinity, Thomas Duke, the "big" alcalde, was summoned from San Felipe. The alcalde (or judge) tied the nuptial knot in good American style, but the contracting parties had to sign a bond to avail themselves of the priest's services to legalize the marriage at the earliest opportunity.

The first and most important number on the program being duly carried out, the next thing in order was the wedding supper, which was the best the market afforded. That being disposed of, the floor was cleared for dancing. It mattered not that the floor was made of puncheons. When young folks danced those days, they danced; they didn't glide around; they "shuffled" and "double-shuffled," "wired" and "cut the pigeon wing," making the splinters fly.

There were some of the boys, however, who were not provided with shoes, and moccasins were not adapted to that kind of dancing floor, and, moreover, they couldn't make noise enough. But their more fortunate brethren were not at all selfish or disposed to put on airs, so, when they had danced a turn they generously exchanged footgear with the moccasined contingent and gave them the ring, and we literally kicked every splinter off that floor before morning.

The fiddle, manipulated by Jesse Thompson's (negro) man Mose, being rather too weak to make itself heard above the din of clattering feet, we had in another fellow with a clevis and pin to strengthen the orchestra. We had a most enjoyable time.

One other wedding to which I was bidden was that of Dr. Angier and Mrs. Pickett. Mills M. Battles, I think, officiated. The wedding, which took place at Captain Bailey's, was a very quiet affair, no dancing or other amusements being indulged in. Another dancing party in which I participated was at Martin Varner's, near Columbia. When we were all assembled and ready to begin business it was found that Mose, the only fiddler around, had failed to come to time, so we called in an old darky belonging to Colnel Zeno Phillips, who performed on a clevis as an accompaniment to his singing, while another negro scraped on a cotton hoe with a case knife. The favorite chorus was:

O git up gals in de mawnin',
O git up gals in de mawnin',
O git up gals in de mawnin',
Jes at de break ob day.

At the conclusion of this the performer gave an extra blow to the clevis, while the dancers responded with a series of dexterous rat-tat-tats with heel and toe.

Ah, those old memories, how they throng around me, bringing up forms and faces long since hidden 'neath the sod. So long ago the events herein narrated occurred that I question if there is now another person living who participated in them.

127

Discussion

1. Why were the bridal couple required to be subsequently married by a priest?
2. Describe some of the dancing customs among the Old Three Hundred.

A Visit to Texas in 1832
by Major George B. Erath

It was on the morning of the first of May that I threw my baggage on one of the ox-wagons then transporting goods from the coast to the interior, and went out as far as the Brazos bottom. The custom was for all wagons to travel together. If the carelessness of one waggoner caused a yoke of oxen to stray at night, the whole train of wagons must wait.

Sometimes a new yoke was lost while the old one was being hunted, and another possibly before the second was found, and so on. Thus our journey was stopped in the Brazos bottom until a party of Mexicans joined us from whom horses were to be obtained.

We all bought horses, and I rode bareback, with a rope around the nose of my animal, while my companions used the saddles which they had brought along with them. And thus we came in two days to San Felipe.

Farming and stock raising, of course, formed the chief industries of the country. But the farming was carried on in a very primitive way, excepting perhaps near the coast, where there were slave owners.

Some families were to be found very comfortably established in double log cabins, with stone chimneys and plank floors. Then again, you saw cabins of logs with the bark on, one room for the whole family and comers and goers. The wind found the crevices between the logs, and sometimes helped the fire to set a wooden chimney to burning. In such a case you could do nothing but climb up on the outside and throw your chimney down, thus leaving the small room more at the mercy of the roaring norther.

School houses of logs were found in the thicker settlements, but seldom was school kept in one for a whole year. The same houses, or the shade of a tree, did very well for a religious service, and preachers of all denominations were passing and repassing.

Much trade was done by way of exchange of property, and cows and calves had got to be used somewhat as a legal tender for ten dollars each. If a man wished to say he had paid fifty dollars for a yoke of steers, very probably he declared that he had paid five cows and calves for it. I heard it said repeatedly in those days that cows and calves were ten dollar bills, and hogs and chickens were change.

129

Discussion

1. How did the early settlers ship their freight?
2. What were some of the inconveniences of traveling in those days?
3. What was the occupation of most of the colonists?
4. Describe their best and their poorest houses, and compare them with the homes that you see to-day?
5. What did they use for churches?
6. What did they use for money?

Frontier Hospitality
by Noah Smithwick

Another type of the old colonists, and one that played an important part in the development of the country, was Thomas B. Bell, who lived up on the San Bernard above McNeal's. I took quite a fancy to him, and gladly accepted an invitation to visit him.

I found him living in a little pole cabin in the midst of a small clearing upon which was a crop of corn. His wife welcomed me with as much cordiality as if she were mistress of a mansion. There were two young children and they, too, showed in their every manner the effects of gentle training. The whole family were dressed in buckskin, and when supper was announced, we sat on stools around a clapboard table, upon which were arranged wooden platters.

Beside each platter lay a fork made of a joint of cane. The knives were of various patterns, ranging from butcher knives to pocket knives; and for cups, we had little wild cymlings, scraped and scoured until they looked as white and clean as earthenware. The milk with which the cups were filled was as pure and sweet as mortal ever tasted. The repast was of the simplest, but was served with as much grace as if it had been a feast, which, indeed, it became, seasoned with the kindly manner and pleasant conversation of those two entertainers. Not a word of apology was uttered during my stay of a day and night, and when I left them I did so with a hearty invitation to repeat visit.

130

It so happened that I never was at their place again, but I was told that in the course of time the pole cabin gave place to a handsome brick house, and that the rude furnishings were replaced by the best the country boasted; but I'll venture to say that the host and hostess still retained their old hospitality unchanged by change of fortune.

Discussion

1. Describe the house in which the host lived.
2. The furniture.
3. The manners of the family.

James Bowie's Indian Fight
by Rezin P. Bowie, 1832

*The writer of this account was James Bowie's brother. In
1832 they were prospecting for gold along the San Saba
River, when they were attacked by Indians. The fighting
lasted only one day, but for seven days longer the Indians surrounded the party, to prevent their escape. The Indians lost
eighty-two men, killed and wounded; the Texans, one killed
and three wounded. This is considered the most desperate
Indian battle in the records of Texas.*

Their number being so much greater than ours, one
hundred and sixty-four to eleven, it was agreed that
Rezin P. Bowie should be sent out to talk to them,
and endeavor to compromise. He started, with David
Buchanan in company, and walked up to within forty
yards of where they had halted. He requested them
in their own tongue to send forward their chief, as we
wanted to talk to him.

Their answer was, "How do you do! How do you
do!" in English, and a discharge of twelve shots, one
of which broke Buchanan's leg. Bowie returned their
salutation with the contents of a double-barreled gun
and a pistol. He then took Buchanan on his shoulder,
and started back to the encampment.

They opened a heavy fire, which wounded Buchanan in two more places slightly, and pierced Bowie's
hunting shirt in several places without doing him any
injury. When they found that their shot failed to bring
down Bowie, eight Indians on foot took after him with
tomahawks. When close upon him they were discov-

ered by his party, who rushed out with their rifles and brought down four of them. The other four retreated to their main body. We returned to our position, and all was still for about five minutes.

We then discovered a hill to the northwest red with Indians. They opened a heavy fire on us, their chief, on horseback, urging them to the charge. When we first discovered him, our guns were all empty with the exception of Mr. Hamm's.

James Bowie cried out, "Who is loaded?"

Mr. Hamm answered, "I am."

He was told to shoot that Indian on horseback. He did so, breaking his leg and killing his horse. We saw him hopping around his horse on one leg with his shield on his arm to keep off the balls. By this time four of our party, being reloaded, fired at the same instant, and all the balls took effect through the shield. He fell and was immediately surrounded by six or eight of his tribe, who picked him up and bore him off. Several of these were shot by our party.

Finding our situation too much exposed among the trees, we were obliged to leave them and take to the thickets. They discovered that we were not to be dislodged from the thicket, and they determined to resort to strategy. They set fire to the dry grass in the prairie, for the double purpose of routing us from our position, and, under cover of the smoke, carrying away their dead and wounded that lay near us.

In the meantime, our party was engaged in scraping away the dry grass and leaves from our wounded men and baggage, to prevent the fire from passing over them. We saw no hope of escape. The fire was coming down rapidly before the wind, flaming ten feet high. What was to be done? We must either be burnt alive or driven into the prairie among the savages.

This encouraged the Indians, and their shouts and yells rent the air, while they fired about twenty shots a minute. The sparks were flying about so thickly that no man could open his powderhorn without running the risk of being blown up. However, we finally came to a determination. We decided that each man should take care of himself as well as he could until the fire reached the ring around our baggage and wounded men, and there it should be smothered with buffalo robes, bear skins, deer skins, and blankets. This, after great exertion, we succeeded in doing.

During the fire the Indians had succeeded in removing all their killed and wounded. It was now sun down, and we had been warmly engaged with the Indians since sunrise. Seeing us still alive and ready for fight, they drew off a hundred yards and encamped for the night.

Discussion

1. Tell what you know of James Bowie.
2. What was he doing at San Saba?
3. Describe the battle.
4. How did Bowie save the party from being burned up by the Indians?

A Smuggling Trip to Old Mexico
by Noah Smithwick, about 1827

*Spain was very unwise in her regulation of the commerce
of her colonies. She would not allow them to trade among
themselves or with other nations except under very burden-
some restrictions. This caused the colonists to be dissatisfied,
and, to evade the bad laws, they often resorted to smuggling
and other forms of illegal trade. When Mexico became independent she retained many of the unwise laws in her prov-
inces, and the people continued to break them. The way this
was sometimes done in Texas is told in this story.*

Under the colonization act, the Texas colonists
were permitted to import, duty free, everything they
desired for their own use; but, in order to carry merchandise into Mexico, they were required to pay a
heavy import duty. The government reserved to itself
the sole right to deal in coffee and tobacco.

Citizens were even restricted in the cultivation of
tobacco. The government, it is said, passed an act
prohibiting any one person from planting more than
one-sixth of a bushel of tobacco seed. Traders had to
pay a heavy duty to get their goods into market, and
a still heavier duty to get their money out; so smuggling was largely resorted to, notwithstanding the
strict patrol maintained along the border. The official
eye, however, was not proof against the dazzle of coin.
There was, therefore, little to fear from that source.
The principal risk lay in the greed of the Mexican
soldiery.

Life in the colonies becoming stale and not being so profitable as I could wish, I sold out my shop down at Bell's Landing (Columbia), invested the proceeds in tobacco, and, in company with Joe McCoy, Jack Cryor, and John Webber, set out for Mexico on a smuggling trip. Altogether we had about 1,000 pounds of leaf tobacco, done up in bales of 100 pounds each, which we packed on mules.

The first town we struck on the Rio Grande was Laredo. Finding that some other trader had got in ahead of us and stocked the market, we proceeded on up the river to find fresh territory. On the way up one of those interminable Texas rains set in, and we were compelled to strike camp and cover up our tobacco.

The weather finally cleared, and we went on up to Presidio del Norte, but the rains had raised the river and there were no boats except rawhide ones, which were not very safe with the river a quarter of a mile wide and running with a swift current. We hid our tobacco out in the chaparral and lay around watching for some chance to cross the river. Over opposite our camp was a goat ranch. Under pretense of getting milk, Cryor and I swam our horses over and reconnoitered. Seeing our designs, the Mexican soldiers concluded to follow our example and investigate us. Their ponies were not strong enough to breast the current and were carried down to a point where the bank was so steep that they could not land.

One soldier was drowned, and the others, after drifting down lower, scrambled out. They found our tobacco and helped themselves to as much as they could conceal, making no attempt to arrest us, as their duty required. To have done so would have necessitated the surrender of the goods to the Mexican government, which they had no intention of doing. Surmising that they proposed returning at their convenience for the bulk of our cargo, we removed it.

We then paid another visit to the goat ranch, and by a little persuasion succeeded in getting a rawhide boat which we took across the river after dark, swimming and towing it. In the same manner we ferried the tobacco over and had it safely hidden before morning.

There was more tobacco than could be disposed of in one little town, so we divided it, Webber and I taking our part up to San Fernando. Cryor and McCoy got in with the alcalde (judge), but the custom house officers learned of the affair and arrested the alcalde. He succeeded in giving the boys warning and they fled, leaving their tobacco buried in the sand.

Webber and I had better luck. Arriving at San Fernando in safety, we hunted up the only white man in the place, John Villars, and made him our confederate. Through his assistance we found safe hiding for our wares with an old Mexican woman, Doña Petra, who enjoyed the distinction of being the widow of a white man, and who was, consequently, the steadfast friend of all Americans. Our staying in her house was, therefore, quite a matter of course, and it caused no suspicion.

We had to dispose of the tobacco in small parcels, which took time. In order to avert any suspicion that an apparently aimless sojourn might arouse, Villars suggested that one of us should be "doctor." American doctors were in demand among the Mexicans, who had no regular physicians. We decided that Webber must shoulder the responsibility. Villars had a store which was the principal advertising medium in the vicinity. Its facilities were ample, and "Dr." Webber's services were soon in requisition. We had taken out a lot of simple medicines for our own needs, consisting for the most part of calomel, quinine, and tartar emetic. As I spoke better Spanish than the "doctor," I accompanied him on his visits, under pretense of being interpreter, but really to see the fun and help him out if he got into deep water.

With an air of importance that would have done credit to a professional, Webber noted the symptoms, shaking his head, knitting his brows, and otherwise impressing the patient with the seriousness of his condition.

138

We sold our tobacco for a good price, getting as high as $2 a pound for some of it, but with what the soldiers stole and the money we necessarily spent, we hadn't more than the law allowed us to take out duty free, so we had no difficulty in leaving the State. Traders who did a large business, though, found the export duty rather heavy and resorted to many devices to evade it.

Discussion

1. In what way did Mexico restrict trade?
2. Tell of her laws about tobacco.
3. What is smuggling? Is it right?
4. In what ways were smugglers sometimes aided by Mexican officials?
5. Is trade restricted in any way by our own laws?

A Little German Girl in Early Texas
by Caroline von Hinueber, 1831-1835

When my father came to Texas I was a child of eleven or twelve years. My father's name was Frederick Ernst. He was by profession a bookkeeper, and emigrated from the duchy of Oldenburg. Shortly after landing in New York he fell in with Mr. Fordtran, a tanner and a countryman of his. A book by a Mr. Duhde, setting forth the advantages of the new State of Missouri, had come into their hands, and they determined to settle in that state. While in New Orleans, they heard that every settler who came to Texas with his family would receive a league and labor of land from the Mexican government.

This information induced them to abandon their first intention. We set sail for Texas in the schooner *Saltillo*. Just as we were ready to start, a flatboat with a party of Kentuckians and their dogs was hitched to our vessel, the Kentuckians coming aboard and leaving their dogs behind on the flatboat.

We were almost as uncomfortable as the dogs. The boat was jammed with passengers and their luggage so that you could hardly find a place on the floor to lie down at night. I firmly believe that a strong wind would have drowned us all. We landed at Harrisburg, which consisted at that time of about five or six log houses, on the 3d of April, 1831. Captain Harris had a sawmill, and there was a store or two, I believe. Here we remained five weeks, while Fordtran went ahead of us and selected a league of land, where now stands the town of Industry.

While on our way to our new home, we stayed in San Felipe for several days at Whiteside's Tavern. The courthouse was about a mile out of town, and here R. M. Williamson, who was then the alcalde, had his office. I saw him several times while I was here, and remember how I wondered at his crutch and wooden leg.

S. F. Austin was in Mexico at the time, and Sam Williams, his private secretary, gave my father a title to land which he had originally picked out for himself. My father had to kiss the Bible and promise, as soon as the priest should arrive, to become a Catholic. People were married by the alcalde also, on the promise that they would have themselves reunited on the arrival of the priest. But no one ever became Catholic, though the priest, Father Muldoon, arrived promptly.

My father was the first German to come to Texas with his family. He wrote a letter to a friend, a Mr. Schwarz, in Oldenburg, which was published in the local newspaper. This brought a number of Germans, with their families, to Texas in 1834.

After we had lived on Fordtran's place for six months, we moved into our own house. This was a miserable little hut, covered with straw and having six sides, which were made out of moss. The roof was by no means waterproof, and we often held an umbrella over our bed when it rained at night, while cows came and ate the moss.

Of course we suffered a great deal in winter. My father had tried to build a chimney and fireplace out of logs and clay, but we were afraid to light a fire because of the extreme combustibility of our dwelling. So we had to shiver.

Our shoes gave out, and we had to go barefoot in winter, for we did not know how to make moccasins. Our supply of clothes was also insufficient, and we had no spinning wheel, nor did we know how to spin and weave like the Americans. It was twenty-eight miles to San Felipe, and, besides, we had no money. When we could buy things, my first calico dress cost fifty cents per yard.

No one can imagine what a degree of want there was of the merest necessities of life, and it is difficult for me now to understand how we managed to live and get along under the circumstances. Yet we did so in some way. We were really better supplied than our neighbors with household and farm utensils, but they knew better how to help themselves. Sutherland used his razor for cutting kindling, killing pigs, and cutting leather for moccasins. My mother was once called to a neighbor's house, five miles from us, because one of the little children was very sick. My mother slept on a deer skin, without a pillow, on the floor. In the morning, the lady of the house poured water over my mother's hands and told her to dry her face on her bonnet.

At first we had very little to eat. We ate nothing but corn bread at first. Later we began to raise cow peas, and afterwards my father made a fine vegetable garden. At first we grated our corn, until father hollowed out a log and we ground it as in a mortar. We had no cooking stove, of course, and baked our bread in the

141

only skillet we possessed. The ripe corn was boiled until it was soft, then grated and baked. The nearest mill was thirty miles off.

The country was very thinly settled. Our three neighbors, Burnett, Dougherty, and Sutherland, lived in a radius of seven miles. San Felipe was twenty-eight miles off, and there were about two houses on the road thither. In consequence, there was no market for anything you could raise, except for cigars and tobacco, which my father was the first in Texas to put on the market. We raised barely what we needed, and we kept it. Around San Felipe, certainly, it was different, and there were some beautiful farms in the vicinity.

Before the war there was a school in Washington, taught by Miss Trest, where the Doughertys sent their daughter, boarding her in the city. Of course we did not patronize it. We lived in our doorless and window-less six-cornered pavilion about three years.

Discussion

1. Who was the first German to settle in Texas with his family?
2. Why did he come to Texas?
3. Describe some of the hardships of the voyage from New Orleans.
4. Describe Harrisburg in 1831.
5. What church did immigrants have to belong to before they could get land in Texas?
6. Describe the home of the family.
7. Describe some of the most common hardships of the settlers.

A Description of Texas in 1834
by Colonel Juan Almonte

Colonel Juan N. Almonte was appointed by the Mexican government in 1834 to make a tour of inspection through Texas. This selection tells in part what he saw.

PART ONE: THE DEPARTMENT OF BEXAR

In 1806 the department of Bexar contained two municipalities, San Antonio de Bexar, with a population of 5,000 souls, and Goliad with 1,400; total 6,400. In 1834 there were four municipalities, with the following population respectively: San Antonio de Bexar: 2,400, Goliad: 700, Victoria: 300, San Patricio: 600, total: 4,000. Deducting 600 for the municipality of San Patricio (an Irish settlement,) the Mexican population had declined from 6,400 to 3400 between 1806 and 1834. This is the only district of Texas in which there are no negro laborers.

Extensive undertakings cannot be entered on in Bexar, as there is no individual capital exceeding $10,000. All the provisions raised by the inhabitants are consumed in the district. The wild horse is so common as to be valued at no more than two dollars and a half when caught. Cattle are cheap; a cow and a calf not being worth more than ten dollars, and a young bull or heifer from four to five dollars. Sheep are scarce, not exceeding 5,000 head. The whole export trade is confined to from 8,000 to 10,000 skins of various kinds, and the imports to a few articles from New Orleans, which are exchanged in San Antonio for peltry and currency.

There is one school in the capital of the Department (San Antonio), supported by the municipality, but apparently the funds are so reduced as to render the maintenance of even this useful establishment impossible. In the whole Department there is but one priest.

PART TWO: THE DEPARTMENT OF THE BRAZOS

The capital of the Department of the Brazos is San Felipe de Austin. The following are the municipalities and towns of the Department, with their population: San Felipe: 2,500, Columbia: 2,100, Matagorda: 1,400, Gonzales: 900, Mina: 1,100, total: 8,000. Towns: Brazoria, Harrisburg, Velasco, Bolivar.

In the population are included about 1,000 negroes, introduced under certain conditions guaranteed by the State government, and although it is true that a few African slaves have been imported into Texas, yet it has been done contrary to the opinion of the respectable settlers, who were unable to prevent it.

The most prosperous colonies of this Department are those of Austin and De Witt. Towards the northwest of San Felipe there is now a new colony under the direction of Robertson; the same that was formerly under the charge of Austin.

In 1833, upwards of 2,000 bales of cotton, weighing from 400 to 500 pounds each, were exported from the Brazos; and it is said that in 1832 not less than 5,000 bales were exported. The corn is all consumed in the country, though the annual crop exceeds 50,000 barrels. The cattle, of which there may be about 25,000 head in the district, are usually driven for sale to

Natchitoches. The cotton is exported regularly from Brazoria to New Orleans, where it pays 2% per cent duty, and realizes from 10 to 10½ cents per pound for the exporter, after paying cost of transport, etc. The price of cattle varies but little throughout Texas, and is the same in the Brazos as in Bexar. There are no sheep in this district; herds of swine are numerous, and may be reckoned at 50,000 head.

The trade of the Department of the Brazos has reached 600,000 dollars. Taking the estimate for 1832 (the settlements having been ravaged by the cholera in 1833), the exports and imports are estimated thus: 5000 bales of cotton, weighing 2,250,000 pounds, sold in New Orleans and producing at 10 cents per pound 225,000 dollars net; 50,000 skins, at an average of one dollar each, 50,000 dollars.

Value of exports, 275,000 dollars (exclusive of the sale of live stock). The imports are estimated at 325,000 dollars.

In this Department there is but one school, near Brazoria, erected by subscription, and containing from thirty to forty pupils. The wealthier colonists prefer sending their children to the United States; and those who have not the advantages of fortune care little for the education of their sons, provided they can wield the axe and cut down a tree, or kill a deer with dexterity.

PART THREE: THE DEPARTMENT OF NACOGDOCHES

The Department of Nacogdoches contains four municipalities and four towns. Nacogdoches municipality has a population of 3,500; that of San Augustine:

145

2,500, Liberty: 1,000, Johnsburg: 2,000, the town of Anahuac: 50, Bevil: 140, Terán: 10; Tenaha: 100; total population: 9,000, in which is included about 1,000 negroes, introduced under special arrangements.

There are three common schools in this Department, one at Nacogdoches, very badly supported, another at San Augustine, and the third at Johnsburg.

Texas wants a good establishment for public instruction, where the Spanish language may be taught; otherwise the language will be lost. Even at present English is almost the only language spoken in this section of the Republic.

The trade of the Department amounts for the year to 470,000 dollars. The exports consist of cotton, skins of the deer, otter, beaver, etc., Indian corn, and cattle. There will be exported during this year about 2,000 bales of cotton, 90,000 skins, and 5,000 head of cattle, equal in value to 205,000 dollars. The imports are estimated at 265,000 dollars.

There are about 50,000 head of cattle in the whole Department, and prices are on a level with those in the Brazos. There are no sheep, nor is there pasturage adapted for them. There are about 60,000 head of swine, which will soon form another article of export.

There are machines for cleaning and pressing cotton in the Departments of Nacogdoches and the Brazos. There are also a number of sawmills. A steamboat is plying on the Brazos River, and the arrival of two more is expected, one for the Neches and the other for the Trinity.

The amount of the whole trade of Texas for the year 1834 may be estimated at 1,400,000 dollars.

Money is very scarce in Texas; not one in ten sales is made for cash. Purchases are made on credit or by barter, which gives the country, in its trading relations, the appearance of a continued fair. Trade is daily increasing owing to the large crops of cotton, and the internal consumption caused by the influx of emigrants from the United States.

Discussion

1. Into what three departments or districts was Texas divided before the revolution?

2. What was the population of the Department of Bexar in 1834?

3. Were the people of Bexar (San Antonio) wealthy?

4. About what was the price of cattle? How does this compare with the price of cattle to-day?

5. Why were horses so cheap?

6. How many public schools were there in Texas in 1834? Were they well attended? Were there any private schools?

7. How many Mexicans were there in the Department of Bexar? How many negroes?

8. What was the population of the Department of the Brazos in 1834? Of the Department of Nacogdoches?

9. How many negroes were there in the two Departments?

10. What did the farmers raise in these two Departments?

11. Where did they sell their crops?

12. What else did they sell besides their crops?

13. Since there was so little money in the country, how did the people trade with each other?

14. Were there any cotton gins in Texas in 1834? Any sawmills? In what part of Texas were they?

Hard Times Before the Revolution
by Captain Jesse Burnam, before 1835

In my twenty-second year I went into the War of 1812. John Hutcheson was my captain and Col. John Coffee commanded the brigade. During this campaign I contracted a disease, and the physicians advised me to seek a warmer climate.

I started with nine families, besides my own, and settled on Red River, at Pecan Point. From there I went to the interior of Texas, stopping for a few months where Independence now is. I had three horses, and brought what I could on them, my wife bringing her spinning wheel and weaving apparatus.

We got out of bread before we stopped. Being too feeble to hunt, I employed an old man to keep me in meat. I had fixed up a camp, so that my family could be comfortable. My man failed to kill a deer, and we were out of food for two days. At last I heard one of my children say, "I am so hungry." I had been lying there hoping to hear the old man's gun. I was too feeble to hunt, but I got up and began to fix my gun slowly. I listened all the time for the old man's gun. I didn't feel as though I could walk, but I started on my first hunt. I had not gone far when I saw two deer, a fawn and its mother. I shot the fawn first, knowing the doe would not run far, then I shot and killed her. "O ho!" said I, "two deer in one day, and my first hunt!" I took the fawn to camp to my hungry children, and took William, my oldest boy, and a horse after the doe. My wife had dressed a skin and made William a shirt, but it lacked one sleeve, so she dressed the fawn skin that day and made the other sleeve.

It was while camped at Independence that I saw my first Indian. I went out to kill a deer and had killed one and was butchering it, when an Indian came up and wanted to take it from me. I would not let him have it, but got it on my back the best I could and started for camp. The Indian began to yell, I suppose for help, but I would have died rather than give the deer up. I thought if there was only one I would put my knife in him and save my gun for another.

I walked along as fast as I could, he pulling at the deer and making signs that he wanted it on his back. I could not put it down to rest, so I walked into a gully and rested it on a bank, the Indian all the time making frightful threats and grimaces. When I got to camp it was full of Indians, and everyone had been dividing meat with them. I told them I would not give them a piece to save my life, and if that Indian came about me I'd kill him.

I stayed in that camp four or five months, and then moved down on the Colorado to what is now the John Holman plantation. All the colony had moved further down, so it was the highest up on the river of any of the settlements, and most exposed to Indians. All my neighbors moved down for protection, and at last I had to go, but did not stay long. I went back and built me a blockhouse to fight from.

We were still out of bread, and it had been nine months since we had seen any. A man from lower down the country came up and told me that he had corn that he had planted with a stick. There were no hoes nor plows in the colony. I gave him a horse for twenty bushels and went sixty miles after it with two horses, and brought eight bushels back. I walked and led my horse. I had prepared a mortar before I left home to beat it in, and a sieve made of deer skin stretched over a hoop and with holes punched in it.

During the time I was without bread, a man who had just come to the country stayed all night with us. He had some crackers and gave the children some. My son took his out in the yard, made him a little wagon, and used the crackers for wheels.

Our honey we kept in a deer skin, for we had no jars, jugs, nor cans. I would take the skin off a deer whole, except having to cut it around the neck and legs, and would tie the holes up very tight. Then I would hang it up by the forelegs, and we had quite a nice can, which we always kept pretty well filled.

My oldest daughter's dresses were worn out before we could get any cotton to spin, and she wore a dress of buckskin. I never wore a deerskin shirt, though there were many that did. I had pants and a hunting shirt made of deerskin. My wife colored the skin brown and fringed the hunting shirt, and it was considered the nicest suit in the colony.

At one time while in camp at Independence I had but six loads of powder. A traveler stopped at my camp, and I asked him if he had any. He said he had. I had a Mexican dollar that Colonel Groce gave to one of the children for dried buffalo meat. I gave it to the traveler and told him to give me as much as he could, for I was nearly out and did not know where to get any. He asked for a tea cup and filled it about two-thirds full. At one time I had twelve loads and killed eleven deer with them.

Discussion

1. Why did Captain Burnam come to Texas?
2. How did he move, and what did he bring with him?
3. How did the colonists often grind their corn?
4. What did they use for jugs and jars?
5. Of what did they sometimes make their clothes?
6. Do you think Captain Burnam was very careful in his statements?

Running the Blockade at Velasco
by Edwin Waller, 1832

Velasco was the Boston Harbor of the Texas Revolution, and the scene of the first chapter in its history. There, too, taxes and duties, unjustly demanded by the government, were the cause of the disturbance.

In 1832 Velasco was a Mexican post, garrisoned by nearly two hundred and fifty men. There were at that time several vessels trading between Velasco and New Orleans, exporting home products and bringing in supplies to barter for Mexican bars of silver and other articles.

Among these vessels was the *Sabine*, which carried out the first cotton ever raised in Gulf Prairie. It was owned by Edwin Waller, then a young man, a native of Virginia. Up to this year no duties or customs had been demanded by government officials from persons engaged in this trade, but it came to their ears that the commerce was becoming profitable, and the commander of the Velasco fort notified the captain of the *Sabine*, Jerry Brown, that he must pay certain duties, and procure a clearance for his vessel from Colonel Bradburn, then commanding at Anahuac, before he would be allowed to sail.

This was demanding impossibilities, as there was no land communication with Anahuac, and this order prevented intercourse by water. Captain Brown reported the facts to Edwin Waller, the vessel's owner, who, in company with Wm. H. Wharton, visited the commanding officer, and offered to pay him a duty of fifty dollars. The official demanded one hundred dollars, and this Mr. Waller refused. He persuaded Captain Brown to agree to "run the blockade."

This was accordingly done, and the first "overt act" of resistance to Mexican authority was committed by Mr. Waller's vessel sailing boldly past the nose of the fort, outward bound.

The sight of this daring violation of his orders excited the Mexican commander to action. Forming his garrison on the bank of the river, he opened a fusilade upon the defiant craft, which did damage only to her rigging. Inspired by this sight, another vessel lying higher up the river, and commanded by Captain Fuller, set sail to follow in the wake of the *Sabine*, which, now being out of range of small arms, was seen crowded with passengers on deck, huzza-ing and shouting in derision and triumph.

This so inflamed the Mexicans that they turned on Captain Fuller's vessel, and opened on her a heavy fire. Before the vessel passed out of range a shot from the Mexicans struck the tiller held by Captain Fuller, wounding him. He immediately called for his rifle, intending to return the salute, when a young man, Spencer Jack, asked leave to fire the gun, and did so with good effect. He wounded a Mexican in the thigh. This worthy sent up such a howl of pain and fright that his comrades ceased firing and gathered in disorder around him. Under this diversion Captain Fuller sailed quietly on his victorious way.

The ball being extracted from the limb of the fallen hero by an American, and the wound proving slight, the warlike ardor of the Mexicans revived, and they

at once arrested, as the originators of this bold dis-
obedience, Colonel Wharton and Edwin Waller, and
conducted them as prisoners inside the fort. Colonel Wharton, with characteristic sagacity and talent,
soon argued himself out of limbo; but Mr. Waller
proving more obstinate, the insulted commander sentenced him to be sent to Matamoras, to be tried by
the authorities there. But, finally, after much trouble,
and principally through the aid of Colonel Wharton,
many good promises being exacted, Mr. Waller was
reluctantly released, and a hollow truce prevailed for
a season.

This occurrence was really the spark which fired
the train of revolution. The first gun sounded when
young Jack fired and wounded the Mexican soldier.

154

Discussion

1. To what place famous in the American Revolution
does Mr. Waller compare Velasco?

2. How was Velasco fortified in 1832?

3. What articles were traded in between New Orleans
and Velasco?

4. Who owned the *Sabine*?

5. Who was its captain?

6. Who was commander at Anahuac?

7. Was the act of the *Sabine* lawful?

8. Describe the way in which the two vessels went by
the garrison.

9. What was done with Mr. Wharton and Mr. Waller?

A Lonely Fourth of July
by Benjamin Rush Milam, 1835

When this letter was written Milam was in prison in Mexico. He escaped in time to reach Texas at the beginning of the revolution. He was killed December 7, 1835, while leading the assault on San Antonio.

Punto Lampasos, July 5, 1835.

Dear Johnson:

I hope you spent the 4th of July pleasantly with your friends who feel some reverence, a bottle of mescal and drank to the Federal Constitution in all parts of America. I had no countrymen to join me, or perhaps I should have done better.

We left Monclova on the 29th of May, and were taken prisoners on the 5th of June, at night. The troops had been watching our march all the last day, and knew the only chance we had to get water. They placed themselves in a position to take possession of our horses as soon as it was dusk.

In this situation we were obliged to surrender to twenty-five men—or savages as we may more properly call them. Captain Galar and Lieutenant Rodriguez commanded the party. They will be long remembered by your humble servant.

We were taken to San Fernando, and kept in close confinement for one week. We were not permitted to write or speak to any person except in the presence of an officer, and then only in the Spanish language.

155

From there we were taken to Rio Grande, where we were treated somewhat better. From Rio Grande we were brought to this place. At present we are under the charge of Colonel Altapa, who is a gentleman, and gives us every indulgence we ask for. From here we expect to be sent to Monterey to stand our trial. I hope to be set at liberty. But all is uncertainty.

In the last ten days two hundred troops have left this quarter for San Antonio, and from the best information I can collect two thousand more will be on their march in a few weeks. Their intention is to gain the friendship of the different tribes of Indians, and if possible to get the slaves to revolt. These plans of barbarity and injustice will make a wilderness of Texas, and beggars of its inhabitants, if they do not unite and act with promptness and decision. The people of Texas will never submit to a dictator.

Yours,
B. R. Milam

Discussion

1. Tell what you know of Colonel Milam.
2. From whom did the Mexicans expect to get help in fighting the Texans?
3. What did Milam think the Texans must do to drive the Mexicans back?

PART FOUR
The Revolution

The Texan Marseillaise
Writer Unknown, March, 1836

*These lines were written by a gentleman near Columbia, on
receiving Travis's call from the Alamo.*

Texians, to your banner fly,
Texians, now your Valor try,
Listen to your country's cry;
Onward to the field.

Armed in perfect panoply,
Marshaled well our ranks must be:
Strike the blow for liberty,
Make the tyrant yield.

Who is he that fears his power?
Who is he that dreads the hour?
Who is he would basely cower?
Let him flee for life.

Who is he that ready stands
To fight for Texas and her lands?
Him his country now commands,
Onward, to the strife.

Small in number is our host,
But our cause is nobly just:
God of battles is our trust
In the dread affray.

The Call to Arms

The first skirmish between the Texans and the Mexicans occurred on October 2, 1835. The Mexicans had come to Gonzales demanding a cannon that the colonists had. It was refused and the Mexicans were driven back to San Antonio. It was expected, however, that they would return immediately with reinforcements, and Wharton was trying to collect a force strong enough to check them again. This proclamation is taken from a circular in the Austin Papers, at The University of Texas.

ARM, ARM; AND OUT.
NOTICE

I am just now leaving for the camp at Gonzales. All who are backward or refuse to go without the best excuse in the world will, in the remorse and bitterness of soul, say to themselves, in after times, the gallant have fallen in vain! My countrymen and friends have won immortal renown—or have bled and fallen fighting my battles, and fighting for the great principle of human liberty, and I was not there. Let all who wish to avoid this heart-rending reflection march immediately to the camp at Gonzales. Every person who cannot go himself, and who withholds a horse or gun from those willing to go will be considered a traitor to his country and therefore infamous. Let no one, however, stop for want of a horse; soldiers who are in earnest have often marched on foot ten times as far as from here to San Antonio.

WILLIAM H. WHARTON,
Agent for the Volunteers.
Brazoria, October 5, 1835

$5,000

WILL be paid to the individual who kills or takes prisoner General Martin Perfecto de Cos, and $500 will be paid for the arrest and detention in close custody of John A. Williams, who, by the most infamous lying and by the production of forged letters from Santa Anna and Cos, prevented sixty-six volunteers from joining their countrymen at Gonzales.

VOLUNTEERS,
Brazoria, October 5, 1835

Discussion

1. State the causes of the battle of Gonzales.
2. Why, in the opinion of Wharton, should all Texans join the army?
3. If a man could not go himself, how could he help others?
4. Why did Wharton want to arrest John A. Williams?

The New Yankee Doodle
by H. Kerr, 1835

*This doggerel was written by a Texan sympathizer in New
Orleans, and was published there, October 19, 1835.*

Santa Anna did a notion take that he must rule
    the land, sir,
The church and he forthwith agree, to publish
    the command, sir,

> *In Mexico none shall be free,*
> *The people are too blind to see,*
> *They can not share the liberty*
> *Of Yankee Doodle Dandy.*

Ye Mexicans henceforth beware, my central plan
    attend to,
My shoulders will the burden bear, no Yankee
    shall offend you,

> *In Mexico, etc.*

Of soldiers now he stands in need, but soldiers
    must be paid, sir,
He then dictates a law with speed, to seize the
    Yankee trade, sir.

> *In Mexico, etc.*

Obedient to their tyrant's will, his myrmidons
    comply, sir.
The Texans see along their coast some vessels
    captured nigh, sir.

In Mexico, etc.

To Vera Cruz they send each prize, each unresist-
    ing man, sir,
Remonstrance, too, is found unwise, it makes the
    foe less bland, sir.

In Mexico, etc.

The Texans say they wont receive the central plan
    at all, sir,
And nobly go to meet the foe with powder and with
    ball, sir.

162   *In Mexico, etc.*

Huzza! for Texas volunteers, we are the boys so
    handy,
We'll teach the Mexicans to fear our Yankee Doodle
    Dandy.

In Mexico, etc.

An Appeal to the Fatherland
by The Council of Texas, 1835

When the revolution began Texas was left without a government, and until one could be formed a committee at San Felipe, called the permanent council, managed affairs. This address asking the people of the United States for help was issued by the council while the Texan army was besieging San Antonio.

SAN FELIPE DE AUSTIN,
October 26, 1835.

*To the Citizens of the
United States of the North:*

The general council of all Texas have determined to address you in behalf of suffering Texas, and to invoke your assistance.

Our citizens were invited to settle Texas by a government having for its model that of the United States of the North. Under that invitation thousands emigrated here, and have subdued a vast and extended wilderness to the purposes of agriculture.

In place of the solitary region inhabited hitherto only by the savage and the beast, they now present a country prosperous in the highest degree, and having inscribed on its face a universal assurance of its future greatness and prosperity.

And now, when we had accomplished all this, when we had just fairly established ourselves in peace and plenty, just brought around us our families and friends, the form of government under which we had been born and educated, and the only one to which we would have sworn allegiance, is destroyed by the usurper, Santa Anna, and a military, central government is about to be established in its stead. To this new form of government the people of Texas have refused to submit.

What number of mercenary soldiers will invade our country we know not, but this much we do know, that the whole force of the nation that can possibly be spared will be sent to Texas, and we believe that we will have to fight superior numbers. But we believe victory in the end will be ours. Only one sentiment animates every bosom, and every one is determined on "victory or death!"

164

Citizens of the United States of the North—we are but one people! Our fathers, side by side, fought the battles of the Revolution. We, side by side, fought the battles of 1812 and 1815. We were born under the same government, taught the same political creed, and we have wandered where danger and tyranny threaten us. You are united to us by all the sacred ties that can bind one people to another. You are, many of you, our fathers and brothers—among you dwell our sisters and mothers—we are alien to you only in country. Our principles, both moral and political, are the same; our interest is one, and we require and ask your aid, appealing to your patriotism and generosity.

We invite you to our country. We have land in abundance, and it shall be liberally bestowed on you, friends. We have the finest country on the face of the globe. We invite you to enjoy it with us, and we pledge to you that every volunteer in our cause shall be not only justly but generously rewarded.

The cause of Texas is plainly marked out. She will drive every Mexican soldier beyond her limits, or the people of Texas will leave before San Antonio the bones of their bodies. We will secure on a firm and solid basis our constitutional rights and privileges, or we will leave Texas a howling wilderness. We know that right is on our side, and we are now marching to the field of battle, reiterating our fathers' motto, "to live free or die."

165

R. R. ROYALL, President.
A. HOUSTON, Secretary.

Discussion

1. What sort of government did Mexico promise those who came to Texas?
2. Why did the Texans object to the change made by Santa Anna?
3. What reasons did the council give for asking aid from the United States?
4. How did they promise to reward those who joined the Texans?
5. What was the permanent council?
6. Where was it in session when this appeal was made?

An Heroic Deed
by J. H. Kuykendall, December 1835

This story was written by Mr. Kuykendall in 1858. It was told to him by one who saw the brave deed performed.

About the last of September, 1835, John Ingram joined the colonial forces at Gonzales, and was in the skirmish with the Mexican troops near that place. He continued in the service until after the reduction of San Antonio, in which he fully participated. During the siege of this town he performed a feat of heroism which is worthy of record.

After the investment of the place had continued some time, a twelve-pounder cannon was received by the Texians, by means of which it was hoped some impression could be made on the Mexican stronghold—the Alamo.

The Texians, favored by a dark night, opened an entrenchment on the right side of the river. Within four or five hundred yards of the Alamo, and at day light the next morning the twelve-pounder, supported by Captain Goheen's company, to which Ingram belonged, began to thunder. The Mexicans were not slow to reply, but in a short time the fire on both sides slackened in consequence of a dense fog which completely concealed every object beyond the distance of a few yards.

After the fog dissolved, the cannonade on both sides was renewed. At length the artillerymen of the twelve-pounder announced that their powder was exhausted. It was immediately asked, "Who will go to

166

the camp for powder?" Without a moment's hesitation Ingram volunteered for the perilous service.

The Texian camp was about half a mile from the battery. Ingram leaped out of the ditch and ran. Five field pieces were bearing on him from the walls of the Alamo, and a thousand infantry were marshaled outside the walls within easy musket range of the intrepid messenger. His course for four hundred yards was over an open field before he could gain the cover of the mill-race which led to the camp.

Simultaneously the five cannon hurled at him their iron missiles. At the next instant a thousand muskets poured a leaden shower around him—still Ingram sped onward. Again, and yet again, a thousand muskets roared in one platoon—but Ingram is still unscathed and safe within the mill-race.

167

He paused not until he reached the quartermaster's tent, where, seizing a keg of powder and placing it on his shoulder, he left as he arrived—running. The same perils awaited him on his return. Three swarm of iron and leaden balls again swept the plain around him, but he seemed to bear a charmed life, for he entered the entrenchment untouched amid the huzzah and congratulations of his fellow soldiers.

Discussion

1. To what siege of San Antonio does this account refer?
2. Do you suppose this description is exaggerated?

Davy Crockett
by John M. Swisher, 1836

The following account was written from memory in 1879.

In January, 1836, David Crockett, who had just left Tennessee, came to Texas for the purpose of assisting the struggling patriots. While on his way to the Alamo he stopped at the Swisher residence, at Gay Hill, to rest after his long journey before beginning his duties as a soldier.

It happened that on the day that Colonel Crockett arrived I had been out hunting with a party of friends. I had killed my second, and, I believe, my last deer, which I tied behind my saddle. I reached home with it about nightfall. Colonel Crockett surprised me by coming out and assisting me in taking it down from the horse. He complimented me highly by calling me his young hunter, and bantering me to a shooting match.

I accepted this proposition, since he offered to shoot off hand and give me a rest. My pride swelled at once. I would not have changed places with the President himself. We tried our skill with the rifle every day he remained with us.

His rifle I well remember. It was ornamented with a silver plate set into the stock, upon which was engraved "David Crockett." He called it "Bessie."

At the time I saw Colonel Crockett, I judge him to have been forty years old. He was stout and muscular, about six feet in height, and weighed from one hundred and eighty to two hundred pounds. He was of a florid complexion, with intelligent gray eyes. He had small side-whiskers, inclining to sandy. His countenance, although firm and determined, wore a pleasant expression. He was fond of talking, and had an ease and grace about him that rendered him irresistible. During his stay at my father's it was a rare occurrence for any of us to get to bed before twelve or one o'clock. He told us a great many anecdotes. Many of them were commonplace and amounted to nothing in themselves, but his inimitable way of telling them would convulse one with laughter.

I shall never forget the day he left us for San Antonio. We watched him as he rode away by the side of his young traveling companion (B. A. M. Smith) with feelings of admiration and regret. We little thought how soon he was to perish—a martyr to the cause of liberty.

169

What Texan does not remember the bravery of that great soul at the massacre of the Alamo, when a few patriots, surrounded by thousands of the enemy, slew ten times their number before they yielded up their lives? Crockett is reported to have been standing calmly, proudly erect, with his clubbed rifle in his hand, dealing death to the foe with unerring aim.

And there he fell—the brave man who sacrificed himself on the altar of Texas liberty. And there his body, with those of the other martyrs, was burned, and his ashes scattered to the four winds of heaven.

Discussion

1. Write a sketch of David Crockett.
2. Describe him as he looked when he came to Texas.

Discussion (continued)

3. Why should Texans always honor his memory?
4. How has the State commemorated his name?
5. Do you think that this account is thoroughly reliable? Give reasons for your answer.
6. How long after the author saw Crockett was it written?

I Shall Never Surrender or Retreat
by William Barret Travis, 1836

Travis's original letter from which this is copied is preserved in the State Library at Austin.

COMMANDANCY OF THE ALAMO
BEJAR, Feb'y 24th, 1836.

To the People of Texas and all Americans in the World.

FELLOW CITIZENS AND COMPATRIOTS—I am besieged, by a thousand or more of the Mexicans under Santa Anna. I have sustained a continual bombardment and cannonade for 24 hours and have not lost a man. The enemy has demanded a surrender at discretion, otherwise, the garrison are to be put to the sword, if the fort is taken. I have answered the demand with a cannon shot, and our flag still waves proudly from the walls. *I shall never surrender or retreat.* Then, I call on you in the name of Liberty, of patriotism and everything dear to the American character, to come to our aid with all dispatch. The enemy is receiving reinforcements daily and will no doubt increase to three or four thousand in four or five days. If this call is neglected, I am determined to sustain myself as long as possible and die like a soldier who never forgets what is due to his own honor and that of his country. VICTORY OR DEATH.

WILLIAM BARRET TRAVIS,
Lt. Col. comdt.

P. S. The Lord is on our side. When the enemy appeared in sight we had not three bushels of corn. We have since found in deserted houses 80 or 90 bushels and got into the walls 20 or 30 head of Beeves.

TRAVIS.

Discussion

1. How many men did Santa Anna have when he began to besiege the Alamo?
2. On what terms did he want the Texans to surrender?
3. Why did Travis not surrender?
4. Why did Travis think the Lord was on his side?
5. Did Travis receive any reinforcements from the Texans?
6. What do you think of Colonel Travis?

The Texian Hunter
by Captain Ruben Marmaduke Potter, 1836

The old hunter described in these lines seems to have been Captain Albert Martin, of Gonzales—at least it was he that led the reinforcements into the Alamo just before it fell. His character is typical of the early frontiersman.

Where murmurs Guadalupe's stream
Along its rocky bed,
Embowered in a live oak grove
There stands a lowly shed,
All mossy grown, for cold has been
Its hearth for many a year.
God rest his soul who once abode
Within that cabin drear;
A brave old Texian hunter he,
All of the prairies wild.

A lonely, strange, untaught old man,
No care nor fear he knew,
So happy in his solitude,
So guileless, kind, and true;
With a heart that, like his rifle good,
Ne'er wavered in its aim,
In weal and woe, to friend or foe,
Its truth was aye the same;
For a fine old Texian hunter bold
Was he who roamed the wild.

173

He seldom sought the busy scene
Where men together dwelt,
Yet kindly towards his fellow man
This mateless woodman felt.
His iron visage smiled, and well
The Arab host he play'd,
Whenever to his green-wood home
A wand'ring footstep strayed,
Like a good old Texian hunter bold,
All of the prairies wild.

When ruffian war dismay'd the land,
In freedom's darkest hour,
Up rose this single hearted man
To brave the invader's power,
And sought those batter'd ramparts where
A fated few opposed,
With fierce despair, the pending shock
Of legions round them closed;
And the stout old Texian hunter burned
With ardor strange and wild.

Said he, "Of laws and governments
I nought can understand;
But I will fight for these green woods
And my adopted land;
Though I'm a lonely forest man,
Nor kindred round me know,
Yet for my native tongue and race
My blood shall freely flow,
As a true old Texian hunter's ought
Who loves his prairies wild."

One night while round the Alamo
Beleaguering thousands lay,
With thirty men he through them charged,
And inward won his way.
Said he, "I thought my bones to lay
Beneath my live oak tree;
But now these doom'd walls shall prove
A nobler tomb for me;"
And the grim old Texian hunter sighed,
"Farewell ye prairies wild."

At dawn, with shout, and cannon's peal,
And charging escalade,
In pour'd the foe, though rank on rank
Their bravest low were laid.
Mid booming shot and bayonets' clang,
Expired that Spartan few;
And there an hundred, ere they sank,
A thousand foemen slew.
There the tough old Texian hunter died
No more to roam the wild.

But in the Elysian hunting grounds
He dwells among the brave
Souls of the free of every age
Who died their lands to save;
And thousands here, when comes the hour,
A fate like his will dare;
For hands and hearts as stout and true
Hath Texas yet to spare,
As the brave old Texian hunter bore
Upon his prairies wild.

I Will Never Give Up the Ship
by James W. Fannin, Jr., 1836

This letter was written by Colonel Fannin about two weeks before he was captured and treacherously murdered by the Mexicans at Goliad.

Goliad, February 28, 1836.

Mr. Jos. Mims:

The news I gave you a few days back is too true. The enemy have the town of Bexar, with a large force, and I fear will have our brave countrymen in the Alamo. Another force is near me. It crossed the Nueces yesterday morning, and attacked a party by surprise under Colonel Johnson, and routed them, killing Captain Pearson and several others after they had surrendered.

I have about four hundred and twenty men here, and if I can get provisions in to-morrow or next day, can maintain myself against any force. I will never give up the ship while there is a pea in the dish. If I am whipped it will be well done, and you may never expect to see me. I hope to see all Texans in arms soon. If not, we shall lose our homes, and must go east of the Trinity for awhile.

Look to our property; save it for my family. If my family arrive, send my wife this letter.

Hoping for the best, and prepared for the worst.

Farewell,
J. W. FANNIN, JR.

Hymn of the Alamo
by Captain Ruben Marmaduke Potter, 1836

The author of this poem was a captain in the United States army, who wrote a great deal about the history of Texas during the revolutionary period.

Rise, man the wall, our clarion's blast
Now Sounds its final reveille!
This dawning morn must be the last
Our fated band shall ever see:
To life, but not to hope, farewell—
Yon trumpet's clang, and cannon's peal,
And storming shout, and clash of steel,
Are ours, but not our country's knell.
Welcome the Spartan's death—
'Tis no despairing strife—
We fall, we die, but our expiring breath
Is freedom's breath of life!

Here, on this new Thermopylae,
Our monument will tower on high,
And "Alamo" hereafter be
In bloodier fields the battle cry!
Thus Travis from the rampart cried,
And when his warriors saw the foe
Like whelming billows move below,
At once each dauntless heart replied,
Welcome the Spartan's death—
'Tis no despairing strife—
We fall, we die, but our expiring breath
Is freedom's breath of life!

They come, like autumn leaves they fall,
Yet hordes on hordes, they onward rush;
With gory tramp they mount the wall,
Till numbers the defenders crush,
Till falls the flag when none remains!
Well may the ruffians quake to tell
How Travis and his hundred fell,
Amid a thousand foemen slain.
They died the Spartan's death,
But not in hopeless strife,—
Like brothers died; and their expiring breath
Was freedom's breath of life.

The Goliad Massacre
by John C. Duval, 1836

On March 19, 1836, by command of General Houston, Colonel Fannin left Goliad with about four hundred and fifty men. He was soon overtaken by the Mexicans under General Urrea, and a battle took place. A number of the Texans were wounded, and it was impossible to continue the march with them, while the men refused to leave them to the mercy of the Mexicans; so it was decided that all should surrender. The Texans claimed that Urrea promised to treat them well and send them back to the United States. But they were taken to Goliad, kept in close confinement for a week, and then, by order of Santa Anna, brutally shot. John C. Duval, who wrote this account, was one of the few who escaped the massacre.

The morning of the sixth day after our return to Goliad we were confined in the mission, where we were so crowded we had hardly room to lie down at night. Our rations, too, about that time, had been reduced to five ounces of fresh beef a day, which we had to cook in the best way we could and eat without salt.

Although thus closely confined and half starved, no personal indignity was ever offered to us to my knowledge, except on two occasions. Once a Mexican soldier pricked one of our men with his bayonet, because he did not walk quite fast enough to suit him, whereupon he turned and knocked the Mexican down with his fist. I fully expected to see him roughly handled for this, but the officer in command of the guard, who saw the affair, came up to him and patting him on the shoulder, told him he was "muy bravo" (very brave) and that he had served the soldier exactly right. At another time one of our men was complaining to the officer of the guard of the rations issued to him, and he ordered one of the soldiers to collect a quantity of bones lying around, and throwing them on the ground before the man, said, "There, eat as much as you want—good enough for gringoes and heretics."

On the morning of the 27th of March, a Mexican officer came to us and ordered us to get ready for a march. He told us we were to be liberated on parole, and that arrangements had been made to send us to New Orleans on board of vessels then at Copano.

This, you may be sure, was joyful news to us, and we lost no time in making preparations to leave our uncomfortable quarters. When all was ready we were formed into three divisions and marched out under a strong guard. As we passed by some Mexican women who were standing near the main entrance of the fort, I heard them say "pobrecitos" (poor fellows).

One of our divisions was taken down the road leading to the lower ford of the river, one upon the road to San Patricio, and the division to which my company was attached, along the road leading to San Antonio. A strong guard accompanied us, marching in double file on both sides of our column. It occurred to me that this division of our men into three squads, and marching us off in three directions, was rather a singular maneuver, but still I had no suspicion of the foul play intended us. When about half a mile above town, a halt was made and the guard on the side next the river filed around to the opposite side. Hardly had this maneuver been executed when I heard a heavy firing of musketry in the directions taken by the other two divisions. Someone near me exclaimed, "Boys! they are going to shoot us!" and at the same instant I heard the clicking of musket locks all along the Mexican line. I turned to look, and as I did so, the Mexicans fired upon us, killing probably one hundred out of one hundred and fifty men in the division. We were in double file and I was in the rear rank.

The man in front of me was shot dead, and in falling he knocked me down. I did not get up for a moment, and when I rose to my feet, I found that the whole Mexican line had charged over me, and were in hot pursuit of those who had not been shot and who were fleeing towards the river about five hundred yards distant. I followed on after them, for I knew that escape in any other direction (all open prairie) would be impossible.

I had nearly reached the river before it became necessary to make my way through the Mexican line ahead. As I did so, one of the soldiers charged upon me with his bayonet (his gun I suppose being empty). As he drew his musket back to make a lunge at me, one of our men coming from another direction, ran between us, and the bayonet was driven through his body. The blow was given with such force, that in falling the man probably wrenched or twisted the bayonet in such a way as to prevent the Mexican from withdrawing it immediately. I saw him put his foot upon the man, and make an ineffectual attempt to extricate the bayonet from his body, but one look satis-

181

fied me, as I was somewhat in a hurry just then, and I hastened to the bank of the river and plunged in. The river at that point was deep and swift, but not wide, and I soon gained the opposite bank.

Discussion

1. What did the Mexicans use as a prison for Fannin's men?
2. What did they think the Mexicans were going to do with them?
3. What did the Mexicans tell them as they were taken out to be shot?
4. Why did the Mexicans separate them into three divisions?
5. Describe the massacre.
6. Who was responsible for the murder of these men?
7. Was there any justification for their killing?

The Battle of San Jacinto
by Sam Houston, 1836

This is General Houston's official report of the battle of San Jacinto.

HEADQUARTERS OF THE ARMY,
SAN JACINTO, April 25, 1836.

To His Excellency, David G. Burnet, President of the Republic of Texas.

SIR: I regret extremely that my situation, since the battle of the 21st, has been such as to prevent my rendering you my official report of the same previous to this time.

I have the honor to inform you that on the evening of the 18th inst., after a forced march of fifty-five miles, the army arrived opposite Harrisburg. That evening a courier of the enemy was taken, from whom I learned that General Santa Anna, with one division of choice troops, had marched in the direction of Lynch's Ferry on the San Jacinto, burning Harrisburg as he passed down.

The army was ordered to be in readiness to march early on the next morning. The main body effected a crossing over Buffalo Bayou, below Harrisburg, on the morning of the 19th, having left the baggage, the sick, and a sufficient camp guard

183

in the rear. We continued the march throughout the night, making but one halt in the prairie for a short time, and with out refreshments. At daylight we resumed the line of march. In a short distance our scouts encountered those of the enemy, and we received information that General Santa Anna was at New Washington, and would that day take up the line of march for Anahuac, crossing at Lynch's Ferry. The Texian army halted within half a mile of the ferry in some timber and were engaged in slaughtering beeves, when the army of Santa Anna was discovered approaching in battle array.

About 9 o'clock on the morning of the 21st the enemy were reinforced by five hundred choice troops, under the command of General Cos; increasing their effective force to upwards of fifteen hundred men, whilst our aggregate force for the field numbered seven hundred and eighty-three.

At half past 3 o'clock in the evening I ordered the officers of the Texian army to parade their respective commands, having in the meantime ordered the bridge on the only road communicating with the Brazos, distant eight miles from our encampment, to be destroyed, thus cutting off all possibility of escape.

Our troops paraded with alacrity and were anxious for the contest. The conscisparity in numbers seemed only to increase their enthusiasm and confidence, and heighten their anxiety for the conflict.

Our cavalry was first dispatched to the front of the enemy's left, for the purpose of attracting notice, whilst an extensive island of timber afforded us an opportunity of concentrating our forces and deploying from that point. Every evolution was performed with alacrity, the whole advancing rapidly in line and through an open prairie, without any protection whatever for our men. The artillery advanced and took station within two hundred yards of the enemy's breastwork, and commenced an effective fire with grape and cannister.

Colonel Sherman with his regiment having commenced the action upon our left wing, the whole line advancing in double-quick time, rung the war cry, "Remember the Alamo!" received the enemy's fire, and advanced within point blank shot before a piece was discharged from our lines.

The conflict lasted about eighteen minutes from the time of close action until we were in possession of the enemy's encampment. We took one piece of cannon (loaded), four stands of colors, all their camp equipage, stores, and baggage. Our cavalry had charged and routed that of the enemy upon the right, and given pursuit to the fugitives, which did not cease until they arrived at the bridge which I have mentioned. Captain Karnes, always the foremost in danger, commanded the pursuers. The conflict in the breastwork lasted but a few moments. Many of the troops encountered hand to hand, and not having the advantage of bayonets on our side, our riflemen used their pieces as war clubs, breaking many of them off at the breech.

The rout commenced at half past four, and the pursuit by the main army continued until twilight. A guard was then left in charge of the enemy's encampment, and our army returned with their killed and wounded. In the battle our loss was two killed and twenty-three wounded, six of them mortally. The enemy's loss was six hundred and thirty killed; wounded, two hundred and eight; prisoners, seven hundred and thirty.

About six hundred muskets, three hundred sabres and two hundred pistols have been collected since the action. Several hundred mules and horses were taken, and near twelve thousand dollars in specie. For several days previous to the action our troops were engaged in forced marches, exposed to excessive rain, and the additional inconvenience of extremely bad roads, illy supplied with rations and clothing; yet amid every difficulty, they bore up with cheerfulness and fortitude, and performed their marches with spirit and alacrity. There was no murmuring.

For the commanding general to attempt discrimination as to the conduct of those who commanded in the action or those who were commanded, would be impossible. Our success in the action is conclusive proof of such daring intrepidity and courage. Every officer and man proved himself worthy of the cause in which he battled, while the triumph received a lustre from the humanity which characterized their conduct after victory.

Nor should we withhold the tribute of our grateful thanks from that Being who rules the destinies of nations, and has in the time of greatest need enabled us to arrest a powerful invader, whilst devastating our country.

I have the honor to be, with high consideration, Your obedient servant,

SAM HOUSTON,
Commander-in-Chief.

Discussion

1. How did General Houston obtain, at Harrisburg, information of Santa Anna's movements?
2. Describe the march of the Texans from Harrisburg to San Jacinto.
3. When did the Texans first encounter the Mexican army?
4. How many soldiers did Santa Anna then have?
5. How many men did General Houston command?
6. Why do you suppose General Houston delayed attacking the enemy?
7. How many additional men did Cos bring to Santa Anna on the 21st?
8. Did General Houston know that Cos was coming?
9. What did General Houston think would be the effect of destroying Vince's bridge?
10. Describe the charge of the Texans.
11. How long did the actual battle last?
12. State the losses of the two armies.
13. What spoils were captured in the Mexican camp?
14. How did the battle of San Jacinto affect the struggle for independence?

A Mexican's Story of San Jacinto
by Pedro Delgado, 1836

Delgado was a colonel on Santa Anna's staff, and he wrote this account in 1837. It is the most vivid description of the battle which we have from the Mexican standpoint.

At daybreak on the 21st, His Excellency (Santa Anna) ordered a breastwork to be erected for the cannon. It was constructed with pack-saddles, sacks of hard bread, baggage, etc. A trifling barricade of branches ran along its front and right.

At 9 o'clock a.m. General Cos came in with a reinforcement of about 500 men. His arrival was greeted with the roll of drums and with joyful shouts. As it was represented to His Excellency that these men had not slept the night before, he instructed them to stack their arms, to remove their accouterments, and to go to sleep quietly in the adjoining grove.

No important incident took place until 4:30 p.m. At this fatal moment, the bugler on our right signaled the advance of the enemy upon that wing. His Excellency and staff were asleep; the greater number of the men were also sleeping; of the rest, some were eating, others were scattered in the woods in search of boughs to prepare shelter. Our line was composed of musket stacks. Our cavalry were riding, bareback, to and from water.

I stepped upon some ammunition boxes, the better to observe the movements of the enemy. I saw that their formation was a mere line in one rank, and very extended. In their center was the Texas flag; on both wings, they had two light cannons, well manned. Their cavalry was opposite our front, overlapping our left.

In this disposition, yelling furiously, with a brisk fire of grape, muskets, and rifles, they advanced resolutely upon our camp. There the utmost confusion prevailed. General Castrillon shouted on one side; on another Colonel Almonte was giving orders; some cried out to commence firing; others to lie down to avoid grape shots. Among the latter was His Excellency.

Then, already, I saw our men flying in small groups, terrified, and sheltering themselves behind large trees. I endeavored to force some of them to fight, but all efforts were in vain—the evil was beyond remedy; they were a bewildered and panic stricken herd.

Then I saw His Excellency running about in the utmost excitement, wringing his hands, and unable to give an order. General Castrillon was stretched on the ground, wounded in the leg. Colonel Trevino was killed, and Colonel Marcial Aguirre was severely injured. I saw also the enemy reaching the ordnance train, and killing a corporal and two gunners who had been detailed to repair cartridges which had been damaged on the previous evening.

Everything being lost, I went—leading my horse, which I could not mount, because the firing had rendered him restless and fractious—to join our men, still hoping that we might be able to defend ourselves, or to retire under the shelter of night. This, however,

189

could not be done. It is a known fact that Mexican
soldiers, once demoralized, cannot be controlled, unless they are thoroughly inured to war.

On the left, and about a musket-shot distance from
our camp, was a small grove on the bay shore. Our
disbanded herd rushed for it, to obtain shelter from
the horrid slaughter carried on all over the prairie
by the blood-thirsty usurpers. Unfortunately, we met
on our way an obstacle difficult to overcome. It was
a bayou, not very wide, but rather deep. The men,
on reaching it, would helplessly crowd together, and
were shot down by the enemy, who was close enough
not to miss his aim. It was there that the greatest carnage took place.

Upon reaching that spot, I saw Colonel Almonte
swimming across the bayou with his left hand, and
holding up his right, which grasped his sword. I stat-
ed before that I was leading my horse, but, in this critical situation, I vaulted on him, and, with two leaps,
he landed me on the opposite bank of the bayou. To
my sorrow I had to leave the noble animal, mired, at
that place, and to part with him, probably forever. As
I dismounted, I sank in the mire waist deep, and I
had the greatest trouble to get out of it, by taking hold
of the grass. Both my shoes remained in the bayou.
I made an effort to recover them, but I soon came
to the conclusion that, did I tarry there, a rifle shot
would certainly make an outlet for my soul, as had
happened to many a poor fellow around me. Thus I
made for the grove, barefooted.

There I met a number of other officers, with whom
I wandered at random, buried in gloomy thoughts

upon our tragic disaster. We still entertained a hope of rallying some of our men, but it was impossible.

The enemy's cavalry surrounded the grove, while his infantry penetrated it, pursuing us with fierce and blood-thirsty feelings. Thence they marched us to their camp. I was bare-footed; the prairie had recently been burnt up, and the blades of grass, hardened by fire, penetrated like needles the soles of my feet, so that I could hardly walk.

After having kept us sitting in camp about an hour and a half, they marched us into the woods, where we saw an immense fire. I and several of my companions were silly enough to believe that we were about to be burnt alive, in retaliation for those who had been burnt in the Alamo. We should have considered it an act of mercy to be shot first. Oh! the bitter and cruel moment! However, we felt considerably relieved when they placed us around the fire to warm ourselves and to dry our wet clothes.

191

We were surrounded by twenty-five or thirty sentinels. You should have seen those men, or, rather, phantoms, converted into moving armories. Some wore two, three, and even four brace of pistols; a cloth bag of very respectable size filled with bullets, a powder horn, a sabre or a bowie knife, besides a rifle, musket, or carbine.

Was this display intended to prevent us from attempting to escape? The fools! Where could we go in that vast country, unknown to us, intersected by large rivers and forests, where wild beasts and hunger, and where they themselves would destroy us?

Discussion

1. What was the condition of the Mexican army when the Texans charged them?
2. Did they attempt to make a strong defense?
3. Describe their panic and the pursuit of the Texans.
4. What did the prisoners think the Texans were to do with them?
5. Would the Texans have been justified in mistreating them?
6. Describe the weapons of the Texans as the Mexicans saw them.
7. Where do you suppose they got most of these weapons?

The Capture of Santa Anna
by Joel W. Robison, 1836

1 was one of a detachment of thirty or forty men
commanded by Colonel Burleson, which left the encampment of the Texas army at sunrise of the morning after the battle of San Jacinto, to pursue the fu-
gitive enemy. Most of us were mounted on horses
captured from the Mexicans. We picked up two or
three cringing wretches before we reached Vince's
Bayou, eight or nine miles from our camp. Colonel
Burleson gave them a few lines in pencil stating that
they had been made prisoners by him, and sent them
back to our camp without a guard.

Colonel Burleson with the greater part of our detachment went up Vince's Bayou—but six of us, to
wit, Sylvester, Miles, Vermillion, Thompson, another
man whose name I have forgotten, and myself, proceeded a short distance farther down the bayou, but,
not finding any Mexicans, turned our course toward
camp. About two miles east of Vince's Bayou, the road
leading from the bridge to the battle-ground crossed
a ravine a short distance below its source. As we approached this ravine we discovered a man standing
in the prairie near one of the groves. He was dressed
in citizen's clothing, a blue cottonade frock coat and
pantaloons. I was the only one of our party who spoke
any Spanish. I asked the prisoner various questions,
which he answered readily. In reply to the question
whether he knew where Santa Anna and Cos were,
he said he presumed they had gone to the Brazos. He

said he was not aware that there were any of his countrymen concealed near him, but said there might be in the thicket along the ravine.

Miles mounted the prisoner on his horse and walked as far as the road—about a mile. Here he ordered the prisoner to dismount, which he did with great reluctance. He walked slowly and apparently with pain. Miles, who was a rough, reckless fellow, was carrying a Mexican lance which he had picked up during the morning. With this weapon he occasionally slightly pricked the prisoner to quicken his pace, which sometimes amounted to a trot. At length he stopped and begged permission to ride—saying that he belonged to the cavalry and was unaccustomed to walking. We paused and deliberated as to what should be done with him. I asked him if he would go on to our army if left to travel at his leisure. He replied that he would. Miles insisted that the prisoner should (not) be left behind, but said that if he were left, he would kill him.

At length my compassion for the prisoner moved me to mount him behind me. I also took charge of his bundle. He was disposed to converse as we rode along; asked me many questions, the first of which was, "Did General Houston command in person in the action of yesterday?" He also asked how many prisoners we had taken and what we were going to do with them. When, in answer to an inquiry, I informed him that the Texian force in the battle of the preceding day was less than eight hundred men, he said I was surely mistaken—that our force was certainly much greater. In turn, I plied the prisoner with diverse questions. I remember asking him why he came to Texas to fight against us, to which he replied that he was a private soldier, and was bound to obey his officers. I asked him if he had a family. He replied in the affirmative, but when I inquired, "Do you expect to see them again?" his only answer was a shrug of the shoulders.

We rode to that part of our camp where the prisoners were kept, in order to deliver our trooper to the guard. What was our astonishment, as we approached the guard, to hear the prisoners exclaiming, "El Presidente! El Presidente!" by which we were made aware that we had unwittingly captured the "Napoleon of the West."

The news spread almost instantaneously through our camp, and we had scarcely dismounted ere we were surrounded by an excited crowd. Some of our officers immediately took charge of the illustrious captive and conducted him to the tent of General Houston.

Discussion

1. Name the captors of Santa Anna.
2. How does Robison say Santa Anna was dressed?
3. Describe the journey to the Texan camp.
4. How did the captors learn that their prisoner was Santa Anna?
5. What was the importance of his capture to the Texans?
6. Would it have been right for the Texans to put him to death in retaliation for the massacres at the Alamo and Goliad? Would it have been prudent?

The Runaway Scrape
by Mrs. Dilue Harris, 1836

In March, 1836, Santa Anna began his advance from San Antonio. General Houston was at Gonzales with only three hundred and seventy-four men. These were not enough to check the Mexican army, so Houston retreated to the Colorado River, hoping to gain time for gathering reinforcements. From the Colorado he found it necessary to fall back to the Brazos. This alarmed the Texans, and whole families began to flee from the country. This wild flight was called the "runaway scrape." The following account of the affair is told by an eye-witness.

196

PART ONE

The people had been in a state of excitement during the winter. They knew that Colonel Travis had but few men to defend San Antonio. I remember when his letter came calling for assistance. He was surrounded by a large army, with General Santa Anna in command, and had been ordered to surrender, but fought till the last man died. I was nearly eleven years old, and remember well the hurry and confusion.

By the 20th of February the people of San Patricio and other western settlements were fleeing for their lives. Every family in our neighborhood was preparing to go to the United States, and wagons and other vehicles were scarce.

By the last of February there was more hopeful news. Colonel Fannin with five hundred men was marching

to San Antonio, and General Houston was on the way
to Gonzales with ten thousand. Father finished planting corn. He had hauled away a part of our household
furniture and other things and hid them in the bottom. Mother had packed what bedding, clothes, and
provisions she thought we should need, ready to leave
at a moment's warning, and father had made arrangements with a Mr. Bundick to haul our family in his
cart. But we were confident that the army under General Houston would whip the Mexicans before they
reached the Colorado River.

On the 12th of March came the news of the fall of
the Alamo. A courier brought a dispatch from General Houston for the people to leave. Colonel Travis and
the men under his command had been slaughtered.
The Texas army was retreating, and President Burnet's cabinet had gone to Harrisburg.

Then began the horrors of the "Runaway Scrape."
We left home at sunset, hauling clothes, bedding, and
provisions on the sleigh with one yoke of oxen. Mother and I were walking, she with an infant in her arms.
Brother drove the oxen, and my two little sisters rode
in the sleigh. We were going ten miles to where we
could be transferred to Mr. Bundick's cart.

We met Mrs. M. She was driving her oxen home.
We had sent her word in the morning. She begged
mother to go back and help her, but father said no.
He told the lady to drive the oxen home, put them in
the cow pen, turn out the cows and calves, and get her
children ready, and he would send assistance.

We went on to Mrs. Roark's, and met five families
ready to leave. We shifted our things into the cart of

Mr. Bundick, who was waiting for us, and tried to rest till morning. Sister and I had been weeping all day about Colonel Travis.

Early next morning we were on the move, mother with her four children in the cart, and Mr. Bundick and his wife and negro woman on horseback. We camped the first night near Harrisburg, about where the railroad depot now stands. Next day we crossed Vince's Bridge, and arrived at the San Jacinto in the night. There were fully five thousand people at the ferry. The planters from Brazoria and Columbia, with their slaves, were crossing. Our party consisted of five white families: father's, Mr. Dyer's, Mr. Bell's, Mr. Neal's, and Mr. Bundick's. Father and Mr. Bundick were the only white men in the party, the others being in the army. There were twenty or thirty negroes from Stafford's plantation. They had a large wagon with five yoke of oxen, and horses and mules, and they were in charge of an old negro man called Uncle Ned. Altogether, black and white, there were about fifty of us. Everyone was trying to cross first, and it was almost a riot.

We got over the third day, and after traveling a few miles came to a big prairie. It was about twelve miles further to the next timber and water, and some of our party wanted to camp; but others said that the Trinity River was rising, and if we delayed we might not get across. So we hurried on. When we got half across the prairie Uncle Ned's wagon bogged. The negro men driving the carts tried to go around the big wagon one at a time until the four carts were fast in the mud. Mother was the only white woman that rode in a cart;

the others traveled on horseback. Mrs. Bell's four children, Mrs. Dyer's three, and mother's four rode in the carts.

All that were on horseback had gone on to the timber to let their horses feed and get water. They supposed their families would get there by dark. The negro men put all the oxen to the wagon, but could not move it; so they had to stay there until morning without wood or water. Mother gathered the white children in our cart. They behaved very well and went to sleep, except one little boy, Eli Dyer, who kicked and cried for Uncle Ned and Aunt Dilue, till Uncle Ned came and carried him to the wagon. He slept that night in Uncle Ned's arms.

PART TWO

The horrors of crossing the Trinity are beyond my powers to describe. One of my little sisters was very sick, and the ferryman said that those families that had sick children should cross first. When our party got to the boat the water broke over the banks above where we were and ran around us. We were several hours surrounded by water. Our family was the last to get to the boat. The sick child was in convulsions.

When we landed the lowlands were under water and everybody was rushing for the prairie. Father and mother hurried on, and we got to the prairie and found a great many families camped there. A Mrs. Foster invited mother to her camp, and furnished us with supper, a bed, and dry clothes. The other families stayed all night in the bottom without fire or anything to eat, and with the water up in the carts. The men drove the horses and oxen to the prairies, and the women, sick children, and negroes were left in the bottom. The old negro man, Uncle Ned, was left in charge. He put the white women and children in his wagon, because it was large and had a canvas cover, and the negro women and children he put in the carts. Then he guarded the whole party until morning.

As soon as it was daylight the men went to the relief of their families and found them cold, wet, and hungry. It took all day to get them out to the prairies. The second day they brought out the bedding and clothes. Everything was soaked with water. They had to take the wagons and carts apart, and it took four days to get everything out of the water.

The town of Liberty was three miles from where we camped. The people there had not left their homes, and they gave us all the help in their power. My little sister that had been sick died and was buried in the cemetery at Liberty. After resting a few days our party continued their journey, but we remained in the town.

We had been at Liberty three weeks, when one Thursday afternoon we heard a sound like distant thunder. When it was repeated, father said that it was cannon and that the Texans and Mexicans were fighting. He had been through the war of 1812, and knew that it was a battle. The cannonading lasted only a few minutes, and father said that the Texans must have been defeated, or the cannon would not have ceased firing so quickly. We left Liberty in half an hour.

We traveled nearly all night, sister and I on horse back and mother in the cart. We were as wretched as we could be; for we had been five weeks from home,

and there was not much prospect of our ever returning. We had not heard a word from brother, mother
was sick, and we had buried our dear little sister at
Liberty.

Our journey continued through mud and water,
and when we camped in the evening fifty or sixty
young men came by who were going to join General
Houston. One of them was Harry Stafford, and his
companions were volunteers that he had brought
from the United States. They camped a short distance
from us.

Suddenly we heard someone calling from the direction of Liberty. We could see that it was a man on
horseback, waving his hat; and, as we knew there was
no one left at Liberty, we thought the Mexicans had
crossed the Trinity. The young men seized their guns,
but when the rider got near enough for us to understand what he said, it was, "Turn back! The Texans
have whipped the Mexican army and the Mexicans
are prisoners! No danger! No danger! Turn back!"

When he reached camp he could scarcely speak, he
was so excited and out of breath. When the young volunteers began to understand the glorious news they
wanted to fire a salute, but father made them stop. He
told them they would better save their ammunition,
for they might need it.

The man showed father a dispatch from General
Houston, giving an account of the battle and saying
that it would be safe for the people to return to their
homes. The good news was cheering, indeed. The
courier's name was McDermot. He was an Irishman
and had once been an actor. During the night he told

many incidents of the battle, as well as of the retreat of the Texan army, and he acted them so well that there was little sleeping in camp that night. The first time that mother laughed after the death of my little sister was at his description of General Houston's helping to get a cannon out of the bog.

Discussion

1. What was the cause of the "runaway scrape"?
2. Describe the horrors of the flight.
3. Were the negroes faithful to their masters during this terrible time?
4. Do you know whether they often deserted their masters during the Civil War?
4. How did the refugees learn of the defeat of Santa Anna?

The Return Home
by Mrs. Dilue Harris, 1836

We were on the move early the next morning. The courier went on to carry the glad tidings to the people who had crossed the Sabine, but we took a lower road and went down the Trinity.

We arrived at Lynchburg in the night, crossed the San Jacinto the next morning, and stayed until late in the evening on the battlefield. Both armies were camped near. General Santa Anna had been captured.

There was great rejoicing at the meeting of friends. Mr. Leo Roark was in the battle. He had met his mother's family the evening before. He came to the ferry just as we landed, and it was like seeing a brother. He asked mother to go with him to the camp to see General Santa Anna and the Mexican prisoners. She would not go, because, as she said, she was not dressed for visiting. She gave sister and me permission to go to the camp, but I had lost my bonnet crossing Trinity Bay and was compelled to wear a table-cloth again. I could not go to see the Mexican prisoners with a table-cloth tied on my head, for I knew several of the young men.

We stayed on the battlefield several hours. Father was helping with the ferry boat. We visited the graves of the Texans that were killed in the battle, but there were none of them that I knew. The dead Mexicans were lying around in every direction.

Father worked till the middle of the afternoon help-ing with the ferry boat, and then he visited the camp. He did not see General Santa Anna, but met some old friends he had known in Missouri. We left the bat-tlefield late in the evening. We had to pass among the dead Mexicans, and father pulled one out of the road, so we could get by without driving over the body.

The prairie was very boggy, it was getting dark, and there were now twenty or thirty families with us. We were glad to leave the battlefield, for it was a grue-some sight. We camped that night on the prairie, and could hear the wolves howl and bark as they devoured the dead.

Early the next morning we were on the move. We had to take a roundabout road, for the burning of Vince's bridge prevented us from going directly home.

We could hear nothing but sad news. San Felipe had been burned, and dear old Harrisburg was in ashes. There was nothing left of the Stafford plantation but a crib with a thousand bushels of corn.

The burning of the sawmill at Harrisburg and the buildings on Stafford's plantation was a calamity that greatly affected the people. On the plantation there had been a sugar mill, cotton gin, blacksmith shop, grist mill, a dwelling house, negro houses, and a stock of farming implements. The Mexicans saved the corn for bread, and it was a great help to the people of the neighborhoods.

We camped that evening on Sims' bayou. We heard that Uncle James Wells was at Stafford's Point, and while mother was talking about him, he and Deaf Smith rode up to our camp. It was a happy surprise.

He had been to our house, and he said everything we left on the place had been destroyed. As Uncle James had fever, mother wanted him to go home with her, but he would not. He said that he had been absent from the army ten days, and must report to headquarters.

Early in the morning we broke camp. The weather was getting warm, and we stopped two hours in the middle of the day at a water hole. When the sun set we were still five miles from home. It was now dark and we traveled slower. The oxen were tired and kept feeding all the time, so that it was 10 o'clock when we got home. We camped near the house. Father said we could not go in until morning.

As soon as it was light enough for us to see we went to the house, and the first thing we saw was the hogs running out. Father's bookcase lay on the ground broken open, his books, medicines, and other things scattered on the ground, and the hogs sleeping on them. When sister and I got to the door, there was one big hog that would not go out till father shot at him. Then we children began picking up the books. We could not find those that Colonel Travis gave us, but did find broken toys that belonged to our dear little sister that died. Through the joy and excitement since the battle of San Jacinto, we had forgotten our sad bereavement.

The first thing that father did after breakfast was to go to the corn field. He had planted corn the first of March, and it needed plowing. He did not wait for Monday, or to put the house in order, but began plowing at once. His field was in the bottom, and he had hidden his plow.

Father had hid some of our things in the bottom, among them a big chest. Mother had packed it with bedding, clothes, and other things we could not take when we left home. After a few days, Uncle and brother hauled it to the house, and that old blue chest proved a treasure. When we left home we wore our best clothes. Now our best clothes were in the chest, among them my old sunbonnet. I was prouder of that old bonnet than in after years of a new white lace one that my husband gave me.

Discussion

1. Describe the condition of the homes in Texas after the Mexicans had plundered them.

2. Mention some of the towns that were destroyed.

206

3. What towns were burned by our people?

4. Why did they destroy them?

5. Did the Texans lose any time mourning over their misfortunes?

No Roof to Call My Own
by Stephen F. Austin, 1836

This letter illustrates some of the hardships which Austin suffered for the sake of Texas.

PEACH POINT, NEAR BRAZORIA.
October 30, 1836.

Mr. Joseph Ficklin—

MY DEAR SIR: I have received several letters from you, and I fear that you have accused me of neglect in not answering them sooner. As an apology, I have to say that on my arrival at Velasco on June 29 I was called up the country on important business, and was in motion during the whole of July and August.

The last of August I was taken sick with fever at the headquarters of the army, and with difficulty reached this place (the residence of my brother-in-law, Mr. James F. Perry). I have had a severe attack, but am now convalescent, though dyspeptic to a great degree, and so debilitated that I am barely able to get about.

I have been told that I have been accused of not treating our Lexington friends with sufficient attention. This has mortified me very much, for I do not merit it. I have no house, not a roof in all Texas, that I can call my own. The only one I had was burnt at San Felipe during the late invasion of the enemy. I make my home where the business of the country calls me. There is none here at the farm of my brother-in-law. He only began to open up the place three years ago, and is still in the primitive log cabins and the shrubbery of the forest.

I have no farm, no cotton plantation, no income, no money, no comforts. I have spent the prime of my life and worn out my constitution in trying to colonize this country. Many persons boast of their three or four hundred leagues, acquired by speculation without personal labor or the sacrifice of years or even days. I shall be content to save twenty leagues, or about ninety thousand acres, acquired very hardly and very dearly, indeed.

All my wealth is prospective and contingent upon the events of the future. What I have been able from time to time to realize in active means has gone as fast as realized, and much faster, for I am still in debt for the expenses of my trip to Mexico in 1833, 1834, and 1835. My health and strength and time have gone in the service of Texas, and I am therefore not ashamed of my present poverty.

In this situation what attentions could I have offered to any one? I held no office, and was then unpopular with the army and many others, on account of the Santa Anna excitement. I mention these things to you—they are not for publication; my only object is to inform my old and esteemed and dearly cherished friends in Lexington of the facts so far as they relate to myself.

I deeply, most deeply, regret that any difficulty or dissatisfaction should have occurred with the volunteers. It is a misfortune, but it ought not and certainly cannot injure the cause of this country.

Please to remember me to my old friends. I hope before March the United States flag will wave all over Texas. God grant it may.

Yours most truly,
S. F. A.

Discussion

1. Was Stephen F. Austin a wealthy man?
2. How much land did he have?
3. How did he get this?
4. What were some of his services to Texas?
5. Who paid his expenses in Mexico?
6. Do you think he was inhospitable?

209

A Mexican's Lament

*The following lines are said to have been adapted about
the time of the revolution by a Mexican inhabitant of San
Antonio from a poem written by Edward Fitzgerald.*

San Antonio! my country! the hour
Of your promising splendor has past,
And the chains which were spurned
In your moments of power
Hang heavily on you at last!

Thou art doomed for the thankless to toil,
Thou art left for the proud to disdain;
And the blood of your sons,
And the wealth of your soil—
Have been wasted—and wasted in vain.

The Mexican riches with taunts have been taken,
Our valor with treason repaid,
And of millions who see us thus sunk and forsaken,
Not one stands forth to our aid.

In the Mexican states, Texas is void;
She is out of the list of the free;
And those we have nourished
And cherished as brothers,
Have at length full possession of thee.

210

PART FIVE
The Republic

The Texian Song of Liberty
by C. D. Stuart

The storm of the battle no longer is o'er us,
Freedom to Texas with glory descends;
The flag of our triumph waves brightly before us,
And conquest her splendor to liberty lends.
Huzza! from our limbs the last fetter has crumbled
And Mexico's pride in the dust has been humbled.

A shout from the banks of Jacinto's bright waters
Goes up with the roar of the storm and the blast;
The voice of her sons and the song of her daughters,
O'er tyranny's chains that are riven at last.
Huzza! never more will our Lone Star surrender
While a true Texan heart is left to defend her.

Then bright be her star and undimmed be the splendor
That links her free name to the love of the world,
and long as one spirit is left to defend her
Let freedom's broad banner be nobly unfurled,
While the lips of her brave and her beautiful thunder,
"No tyrant shall trample our liberty under."

The Keenest Blade at San Jacinto
by David G. Burnet, 1838

Colonel Wharton, a brother of William H. Wharton was one of the earliest advocates of a declaration of independence from Mexico, and took a prominent part throughout the revolution. After the revolution he was for a time Secretary of the Navy. In 1838 he was a member of the Texan Congress, from Brazoria. It was in this year that he died.

The keenest blade on the field of San Jacinto is broken!—the brave, the generous, the talented John A. Wharton is no more! His poor remains lie cold and senseless before you, wrapt in the habiliments of the grave. A braver heart never died. A nobler soul, more deeply imbued with the pure and fervent spirit of patriotism, never passed its tenement of clay to the more genial realms of immortality. He was young in years, and at the very threshold of his fame; and still it is a melancholy truth, to which every heart in this assembly will respond in painful accordance, that a mighty man has fallen amongst us. Many princes of the earth have perished in their prime, surrounded with all the gorgeous splendors of wealth and power, and their country has suffered no damage. But surely it will be engraven on the tablets of our history, that Texas wept when Wharton died.

The brief time permitted us to linger about his untenanted form is insufficient to recite the testimonials of his gallantry. It is enough to say that he was distinguished on the field of San Jacinto, for there were no recreants there. All had strung their chafed

213

and dauntless spirits to the high resolve of liberty or death. And he who could make himself conspicuous on such a battlefield was something more than hero, a hero among heroes!—for never in the annals of war did braver hearts or stouter hands contend for liberty.

To you, soldiers, he was endeared by many ties. You have shared with him the toils and privations of an arduous and protracted campaign. You have witnessed his devotion to his country. You have marked his gallant bearing, when the shock of arms first sounded on the plain, and the war cry of "Alamo!" carried terror and dismay into the camp of the bloody homicides of Goliad. Behold your brother in arms! a cold, silent, prostrate corpse.

No more shall the din of war arouse his martial spirit to deeds of high emprise. That lifeless clay would heed it not; for the bright spirit that lately animated and adorned it has passed triumphantly beyond the narrow bourne of mortal strifes to that blessed region where "wars and rumors of wars are never heard."

To the poor he was kind, generous, and "open as day in melting charity." To the weak and friendless he was a ready refuge and defense. Of him it may be said with great propriety, in the language of the poet, that: "All the oppressed who wanted strength, had his at their command."

Discussion

1. What part did John A. Wharton take early in the revolution?
2. What office did he fill after the revolution?
3. Make a list of the good qualities assigned to him by Judge Burnet.

The Council House Fight
by Mary A. Maverick, 1840

Mrs. Maverick, wife of Samuel Maverick, came to Texas in 1838. She was an eye-witness of the battle which she here describes. It is one of the most famous conflicts that occurred between the Comanches and the Texans.

On Tuesday, March 19, 1840, sixty-five Comanches came into the town [San Antonio] to make a treaty. They brought with them, and reluctantly gave up, Matilda Lockhart, whom they had captured with her younger sister, in December, 1838, after killing two others of the family. The Indian chiefs and men proceeded to the courthouse where they met the city and military authorities. Captain Tom Howard's company was at first in the courthouse yard. The Indian women and boys came in there, too, and remained during the pow-wow. The young Indians amused themselves shooting arrows at pieces of money put up by some of the Americans.

215

I went over to Mrs. Higginbotham's, whose place adjoined the courthouse yard, and we watched the young savages through the picket fence.

This was the third time the Indians had come for a talk, pretending to seek peace and trying to get ransom money for their American and Mexican captives. Their present proposition was that they should be paid an enormous price for Matilda Lockhart and a Mexican they had just given up, and that traders be sent with paint, powder, flannel, blankets, and such other articles as they should name, to ransom the other captives. This course had been adopted once before, and when the traders reached the Indian camp the smallpox broke out amongst them. They killed the traders, saying that they had introduced the disease to kill off the Indians. After the slaughter they retained both the captives and the goods.

Now, the Americans answered, "We will keep four or five of your chiefs, and the others of you shall go to your nation and bring all the captives here; then we will pay all you ask for them. Meanwhile, the chiefs that we hold we will treat as brothers, and not one hair of their heads shall be injured. This we have determined upon, and if you resist our soldiers will shoot you down."

216

The Comanches instantly, and as one man, raised a terrific war-whoop, drew their bows and arrows, and commenced firing with deadly effect, at the same time trying to break out of the council hall.

The order "Fire!" was given by Captain Howard, and the soldiers fired into the midst of the crowd. The first volley killed several Indians and two of our own people. Soon all rushed out into the public square, the civilians to procure arms, the Indians to escape, and the soldiers in close pursuit.

The Indians generally struck out for the river. Soldiers and citizens pursued and overtook them at all points. Some were shot in the river and some in the streets. Several hand-to-hand encounters took place, and some Indians took refuge in stone houses and closed the doors.

When the deafening war-whoop sounded in the courtroom, it was so loud and shrill, so sudden and inexpressibly horrible, that we women, looking through the fence cracks, for a moment could not understand its meaning. The Indian boys, however, instantly recognized its meaning, and turning their arrows upon Judge Robinson and other gentlemen standing near by, slew the judge on the spot.

We fled precipitately, Mrs. Higginbotham into her house and I across the street to my Commerce Street door. Two Indians rushed by me on Commerce Street, and another reached my door and turned to push it just as I slammed it to and beat down the heavy bar.

I rushed into the house and in the north room found my husband and my brother Andrew sitting calmly at a table inspecting some plats of surveys. They had heard nothing! I soon gave them the alarm, and hurried by to look after my boys. Mr. Maverick and Andrew seized their arms. Mr. Maverick rushed into the street and Andrew into the backyard where I was, now shouting at the top of my voice, "Here are Indians! Here are Indians!"

Three Indians had gotten in through the gate on Soledad Street and were making towards the river. One had stopped near Jinny Anderson, our cook, who stood bravely in front of the children—mine and hers. She held a great stone in her hands, lifted above her head, and I heard her cry out to the Indian, "G'way from heah, or I'll mash your head with this rock!"

The Indian seemed regretful that he hadn't time to dispatch Jinny and her brood; but his time was short, and, pausing but a moment, he turned and rushed down the bank, jumped into the river, and struck out for the opposite shore.

As the Indian hurried down the bank my brother ran out in answer to my calls. While the Indian was swimming, Andrew drew his unerring bead on him. Another Indian was climbing the opposite bank and was about to escape, but Andrew brought him down also. Then Andrew rushed up Soledad Street, looking for more Indians.

Not one of the sixty-five Indians escaped. Thirty three were killed and thirty-two taken prisoners.

Discussion

1. What was the cause of the Council House fight?
2. Do you think the Texans were to blame in bringing on the fight?
3. How many Indians were killed?
4. How many captured?

Austin in 1840
by an immigrant

*This description tells of the crude beginnings in 1840 of
what is now (1904) a beautiful city of twenty-five thousand
inhabitants, and the site of a large university and of one of
the most beautiful capitol buildings in the United States.*

About two or three o'clock we came in sight of the
city of Austin, the new capital of the Republic. The
first object that attracted our attention was a white
house, designated as the residence of the president.

"On that spot," said a traveler on horseback by our
side, pointing to the president's house, "I, for the first
time, saw a buffalo. It was in May last, and he was
feeding in perfect quietness."

219

A beautiful spot The city commands from its front
a fine view of a beautiful prairie, extending to the Colorado on the south. On the prairie extending more
than half a mile from east to west, are seen clusters
of small houses, mostly of logs, and timbers either in
heaps, or just begun to be laid as foundations of future dwellings and places of business.

In a beautiful valley, extending at nearly right angles
from the river, some distance towards the extreme
north part of the city, is a broad street, called Congress Avenue, passing through the whole extent of the
contemplated city. On this street are erected temporary accommodations for the several secretaries and
heads of departments. At a little to the westward and
nearly opposite the mansion of the president, stands
a neat white building, at present occupied by the two

houses of congress. Farther south on the same street, and not far from the center, are found the hotels, stores, and most densely built part of the town.

At this time the population is estimated at about one thousand souls, and is rapidly increasing. Some idea of the mushroom rapidity of its growth may be formed from the fact that, less than six months since, not a stone was laid, or a blow struck upon a piece of timber, nor even a tent spread.

Scattered through the town we discovered a number of Indians who seemed to have visited the place for purposes of trade, as some of their horses carried packs of buffalo and other skins. Their dress and appearance betokened little resembling refinement or civilization. Numbers of the men seemed to possess no other clothing than a slight cloth girdled about their waists. They were said to be Tonkawas and Lipans, two small tribes who are generally hostile to the Comanches, and of course friendly with the whites. They seem to be regarded with but little respect as enemies, but are very valuable as guides and scouts in searching for the trails and hiding places of foes. The friendly relations and small numbers of the Indians prevent any fear from them, and hence they come and go at any of the towns and settlements without awakening fear or suspicion.

Discussion

1. What were some of the crude conditions at Austin in 1840?

2. How were the Lipan and Tonkawa Indians regarded at that time?

3. Were they always regarded thus?

4. Did the writer of this piece make a careful estimate of the size of Austin?

5. Ask a number of the citizens what is the size of your own town. Compare their estimates with the figures given in the last census report.

A Texian Camp Song
Writer Unknown, 1841

*This poem illustrates the spirit of many of the volunteers
who came from the United States during and after the
revolution.*

Our rifles are ready,
And ready are we;
Neither fear, care, nor sorrow
In this company.
Our rifles are ready
To welcome the foe,
So away o'er the Sabine,
For Texas we go.

For Texas, the land
Where the bright rising star
Leads to beauty in peace,
And to glory in war.
With aim never erring
We strike down the deer,
We chill the false heart
Of the Red Man with fear.

The blood of the Saxon
Rolls full in the veins
Of the lads that must lord
O'er Mexico's plains—
O'er the plains where the breeze
Of the South woos the flowers,
As we press those we love
In their sweet summer bowers.

One pledge to our loves!
When the battle is done,
They shall share the broad lands
Which the rifle has won.
No tear on their cheeks—
Should we sleep with the dead,
There are rovers to follow
Who will still "go ahead;"
Who will still "go ahead"
Where the bright, rising star
Leads to beauty in peace,
And to glory in war.

Captured by Comanches
by Rebecca J. Gilleland Fisher, 1840

Mrs. Fisher, who here tells her terrible experience, is at present (1904) living in Austin. Her story illustrates some of the dangers of frontier life in early Texas.

My parents, Johnstone and Mary Barbour Gilleland, were living in Pennsylvania, surrounded with everything to make life pleasant, when they became so enthusiastic over the encouraging reports from Texas that they concluded to join the excited throng and wend their way to this, the supposed "Eldorado of the West." They hastily, and at great sacrifice, disposed of their property, and, leaving their home near Philadelphia, set sail for Galveston with their three children. Not being used to the hardships and privations of frontier life, they were ill prepared for the trials which awaited them. I know not the date of their arrival. They moved to Refugio county, near Don Carlos Ranch, which proved to be their last earthly habitation.

My father belonged to Captain Tumlinson's company for some months, and when not in active warfare was engaged in protecting his own and other families, removing them from place to place for safety. They frequently had to flee through blinding storms, cold and hungry, to escape Indians and Mexicans. The whole country was in a state of excitement. Families were in constant danger and had to be ready at any moment to flee for their lives.

The day my parents were murdered was one of those days which youth and old age so much enjoy. It was in strange contrast to the tragedy at its close. We were only a few rods from the house. Suddenly the war whoop of the Comanche burst upon our ears, sending terror to all hearts. My father, in trying to reach the house for weapons, was shot down, and near him my mother, clinging to her children and praying God to spare them, was also murdered. As she pressed us to her heart we were baptized in her precious blood.

We were torn from her dying embrace and hurried off into captivity, the chief's wife dragging me to her horse and clinging to me with a tenacious grip. She was at first savage and vicious looking, but from some cause her wicked nature soon relaxed, and folding me in her arms, she gently smoothed back my hair, indicating that she was very proud of her suffering victim.

225

A white man with all the cruel instincts of the savage was with them. Several times they threatened to cut off our hands and feet if we did not stop crying. Then the woman, in savage tones and gestures, would scold, and they would cease their cruel threats. We were captured just as the sun was setting and were rescued the next morning.

During the few hours we were their prisoners, the Indians never stopped. Slowly and stealthily they pushed their way through the settlement to avoid detection, and just as they halted for the first time the soldiers suddenly came upon them, and firing commenced. As the battle raged, the Indians were forced to take flight. Thereupon they pierced my little brother through the body, and, striking me with some sharp instrument on the side of the head, they left us for dead, but we soon recovered sufficiently to find ourselves alone in that dark, dense forest, wounded and covered with blood.

Having been taught to ask God for all things, we prayed to our Heavenly Father to take care of us and direct us out of that lonely place. I lifted my wounded brother, so faint and weak, and we soon came to the edge of a large prairie, when as far away as our swimming eyes could see we discovered a company of horsemen. Supposing them to be Indians, frightened beyond expression, and trembling under my heavy burden, I rushed back with him into the woods and hid behind some thick brush. But those brave men, on the alert, dashing from place to place, at last discovered us. Soon we heard the clatter of horses' hoofs and the voices of our rescuers calling us by name, assuring us they were our friends who had come to take care of us. Lifting the almost unconscious little sufferer, I carried him out to them as best I could. With all the tenderness of women, their eyes suffused with tears, those good men raised us to their saddles and hurried off to camp, where we received every attention and kindness that man could bestow.

I was seven years of age when my parents were murdered. Fifty-nine years have passed since then, and yet my heart grows faint as that awful time passes in review. It is indelibly stamped upon memory's pages and photographed so deeply upon my heart that time with all its changes can never erase it.

The Santa Fe Expedition
by George Wilkins Kendall, 1841

After the revolution, Texas claimed that her territory was bounded on the west by the Rio Grande as far as its source. This boundary would have given her the richest part of what is now New Mexico. Santa Fé was the most important town in this district, and President Lamar wanted to annex it, if possible; or, if he could not do this, he wanted to establish friendly trading relations with it. The Mexicans misunderstood the object of the expedition, captured a number of the Texans, and carried them to Mexico, where they were put in prison.

In the early part of April, 1841, I determined upon making a tour of some kind on the great western prairies. I was moved by the hope of correcting a derangement of health, and by a strong desire to visit regions inhabited only by the roaming Indian, as well as to take part in the wild excitement of buffalo hunting and other sports of the border.

While canvassing the chances and merits of a trip of this kind, I met with Major George T. Howard, then in New Orleans purchasing goods for the Texan Santa Fe Expedition. Of the character of this enterprise I at once made inquiry. Major Howard informed me that it was commercial in its intentions, the policy of the President of Texas being to open a direct trade with Santa Fe by a route known to be much nearer than the great Missouri Trail. To divert this trade was certainly the primary and professed object; but

227

that General Lamar had a further intention—that of
bringing so much of New Mexico as lies upon the
Texan side of the Rio Grande under the protection of
his government—I did not know until I was upon the
march to Santa Fe.

He was led to think of this plan by a well-founded
belief that nine-tenths of the inhabitants were discon-
tented under the Mexican yoke, and anxious to come
under the protection of the Texas flag, to which they
really owed fealty. The causes which influenced him
in this belief were assurances from New Mexico—positive assurances—that the people would hail the coming of an expedition with gladness, and at once declare allegiance to the Texan government.

Texas claimed as her western boundary the Rio
Grande; the inhabitants within that boundary
claimed the protection of Texas. Was it anything but a
duty, then, for the chief magistrate of Texas to afford
all its citizens such assistance as was in his power?

The time had now arrived, so thought the rulers
of Texas, when the citizens of her farthest borders
should be brought into the common fold—and, with
the full belief in their readiness and willingness for
the movement, the Texan Santa Fe Expedition was
originated. On its arrival at the destined point, should
the inhabitants really show a disposition to declare allegiance to Texas, the flag of the single star Republic
was to be raised on the government house at Santa
Fe; but if not, the Texan commissioners were mere-
ly to make such arrangements with the authorities
as would best tend to the opening of trade, and then
retire. The idea, which has obtained belief to some

228

extent in the United States, that the first Texan Santa Fe pioneers were but a company of marauders sent to burn, slay and destroy in a foreign and hostile country, is so absurd as not to require contradiction. The attempt to conquer a province, numbering some one hundred and fifty thousand inhabitants, was a shade too quixotic to find favor in the eyes of the three hundred and twenty odd pioneers who left Texas, encumbered with wagons, merchandise, and the implements of their different trades and callings.

The expedition was unfortunate, and, as a natural consequence, the censorious world has said that it was conceived in unwise policy.

Discussion

1. What did Major Howard claim was the object of the Santa Fe Expedition?

2. What other object did President Lamar have?

3. What reasons had he for thinking that his plan would succeed?

4. What incorrect notion of the purposes of the expedition have some people had?

229

A Western Leather Stocking
by George Wilkins Kendall, 1841

Mr. Kendall here describes one type of Western frontiersmen of early days.

While "nooning" on our third day's march from San Antonio, I set off, in company with an original chap named Tom Hancock, in the hope of being able to kill a deer. This fellow Hancock was a perfect "character," as much so as the celebrated Leather Stocking of Cooper's novels.

In person he was spare and gaunt, with a loose, shambling carriage of body that ill betokened the firm set muscles and iron powers of endurance he really possessed. When standing erect, his height may have been five feet seven or eight inches; but he had a lazy, listless stoop, which shortened his stature two or three inches and gave him the appearance of being misshapen and round shouldered. His limbs were anything but symmetrical, and seemed to hang dangling about him—this on ordinary occasions; but when his muscles were nerved, and his body straightened in the excitement of adventure, it was then that Tom appeared in his true light, a wiry, knotted embodiment of action, power, and determination.

Decidedly the best point about him was his eye, a small, twinkling orb, of no definable color, but which never allowed any object within the farthest reach of human vision to pass unnoticed. And yet, one might journey with him for days and never suppose that he was looking at or for anything. But not a footprint, not a trail, escaped the notice of that quiet, rolling eye. Tom could tell you the animal that made it, the direction in which it was going, and the time that had elapsed since it was impressed upon the surface of the prairie.

In every species of backwoods, border, and prairie strategy, Hancock had his gifts, and they were such as have been vouchsafed to but few. An Indian he could circumvent and out-maneuver at his own games; and at killing every kind of animal known in the woods or on the prairies, at fishing, or at "lining" bees, the oldest and best hunters acknowledged Tom's supremacy. He could lie closer to the ground, creep farther, expose less of his person, and get nearer deer, bear, buffalo, or an enemy's camp, than any other man. These qualities made him invaluable, not only as a mere provider of meat for camp, but as a spy.

231

He had been in frays numberless with the Mexicans, as well as Indians, and invariably performed some exploit that would furnish his companions with a topic for conversation. He had been a prisoner among the Comanches, but had got away from them—indeed, had made hairbreadth 'scapes innumerable. Yet he never, on any occasion, boasted of his feats—never even spoke of them.

Tom's ordinary weapon, and the one upon which he most prided himself, was a long, heavy, flintlock rifle of plain and old-fashioned workmanship, for he could not be made to believe in percussion caps and other modern improvements.

Such is a rough and imperfect picture of Tom Hancock—of one nurtured amid the solitudes of the woods and prairies—whose days had been spent in the excitements and dangers of the chase or of Indian frays, and whose nights had been passed amid serenades of wolves and owls.

He had been hired at San Antonio by Mr. Falconer—not as his servant, for Tom would scorn being the washer of dishes or brusher of clothes for any man—but simply to accompany the Santa Fe Expedition. His obligations to Mr. Falconer extended this far—he was to find him if lost, and to keep him in provisions should other supplies fail.

Discussion

1. Describe Tom Hancock's appearance.
2. Tell about his keen sight.
3. His prowess.
4. His gun.
5. His pride.

Old Time Schools in Texas
by M. M. Kenney, 1835-1842

The first school that I remember, though I didn't attend it, was in Austin's colony in 1835. It was taught by an Irishman named Cahill. My older brother was one of the pupils of that primitive academy. It was distant about two miles from our house, and the way was through the woods without any road or path. When he started to school, our father was absent and mother went with him, carrying a hatchet to blaze the way.

Of the discipline of the school and its studies, I only know that my brother, in relating the experience of several of the boys, made the impression on me that the rod was not spared. My recollection of the books is reduced to the arithmetic. In this the primitive rules were illustrated by engravings; that for subtraction being a bunch of grapes, showing in successive pictures how, after eating two, three, etc., so many remained. Thinking that this must have been the work of a little boy like myself, I put the lesson into practice by purloining from a basket of "forbidden fruit" and then producing the arithmetic as authority for the appropriation—a sally which mother allowed to condone the little sin.

The next school was at the same place in 1838 or 1839, taught by Mr. Dyas, an old Irish gentleman, and I think a regular teacher by profession. The session was three or four months and the studies mis-

233

cellaneous, but the discipline was exact. He had an assortment of switches set in grim array over the great opening where the chimney was to be when the school house should be completed. On one side was the row for little boys, small straight and elastic, from a kind of tree which furnished Indians with arrows and the schoolmaster with switches at the same time.

I remember thinking of the feasibility of destroying all that kind of timber growing near the school house. My terror was a little red switch in that rank which I caught too often, usually for the offense of laughing.

The larger switches were graded, partly by the size of the boys and partly by the gravity of the offense, the gravest of which was an imperfect lesson. The third size of rods was of hickory, tough sticks, which he did not use on little boys, but which he did use on the larger scholars, without the least hesitation or reserve, if they failed to get the appointed lesson.

As for studies, we all had Webster's spelling book, and were classed according to our proficiency in that great classic. The last few pages contained some stories and fables, intended for reading lessons. They were illustrated, and the last one had a picture of a wolf, by some accident well executed—a fact which tended to establish the book in our estimation, because we saw wolves every day. "The picture of the wolf in the spelling book" thus became the synonym of graduation. Whether it originated with us or not I do not know, but the expression was long used in a humorous sense as equivalent to a diploma, and when it was said of a boy that he had studied to "the picture of the wolf in the spelling book" his ability was not afterward questioned.

The pupils brought such books as they happened to have, and one young man had *Robinson Crusoe* for his reading book. His readings interested me greatly, but I fear that my attention was given to the adventures of Crusoe rather than to the teacher's precepts for reading well. Several had Weems's *Life of Washington*, in which the story of the little hatchet and the cherry tree was most impressed upon our memory. There were no classes in arithmetic. Each boy ciphered through his textbook as fast as he could, and the stern teacher pointed to the errors with the switch held like a pen, and a wag of the head that meant correction.

We walked morning and evening to school, carrying our dinners in tin pails, and milk in a variety of bottles. Some had clear glass, some green glass wine bottles, and some black or junk bottles. A contention having arisen among the boys as to the relative strength of these wares, it was submitted to the test of striking the bottles together, the boys whose bottles were broken admitting defeat—which, in some vague way, I thought involved humiliation—while the boys whose bottles survived the conflict vaunted their victories. Bottles were of vastly more value then than now, and some of the small boys having cried about their loss, brought in the teacher with his switches to umpire the game, and he decided to administer impartial fate.

The *Robinson Crusoe* boy, of whom I have spoken, one day took it into his head to teach us some arithmetic. There were five cows grazing by the side of the path,

235

and he maintained that there were fourteen, proving it in this way: There are four in a bunch on the right and one by itself on the left; four on the right and one on the left make fourteen. We admitted the correctness of the numeration in the abstract, but could not see the cows in the concrete.

"Well," said he, "apply your arithmetic; when you buy cattle count in the old way, but when you sell cattle numerate them."

In the fall and winter of 1841 and 1842 another school house materialized as far to the east as the other was to the west, nearly two miles from home. It was a neat log house in a grove in the prairie, with no spring near, but the patrons substituted a well. The house was an improvement on the other, in that it had shutters to windows and door; glass was still far in the future. We had also a chimney and wide fireplace where we kept a roaring log heap in cold weather, when the neighbors brought wood on their wagons (which they did turn about), and a flaming, crackling brush heap when we had to bring fuel by hand from the neighboring woods.

Our teacher tried to teach mental arithmetic orally to the school, assembled, as the legislative journals say, "in committee of the whole." The teaching was carried on by sudden questions, which we were expected to answer in the style of an exclamation. He was more successful with his singing geography, where, beginning at Baffin's Bay and going south around the continents of the western hemisphere, the names of all the bays were chanted in a unity of discord and loud voices, the pupils following with finger on map, and the chant continuing until the last one had found the bay as well as the name. Then followed the capes, islands, mountains, rivers, etc.

Discussion

1. Describe a primitive Texas school house.
2. Name some of the books used.
3. How were spelling and arithmetic taught?
4. What readers were used?
5. What is meant by "singing" geography?
6. Compare this school with the one you attend.

Up, Men of Texas, to the Fight
Writer Unknown, 1842

These verses were written at Richmond, Texas, March 27,
1842, the anniversary of Fannin's massacre. 'They were oc-
casioned by some raids which the Mexicans had just made on
San Antonio and Goliad.

Ye men of Texas, can you see
   Your swarthy foemen coming on,
And know that God has made you free,
   By San Jacinto's battle won?
Can you look on with careless eye,
   Regardless of your sacred right,
Or strive a shameless peace to buy?
   Up, men of Texas, to the fight!

Oh, bitter shame, and deep disgrace!
   Shall Texas' star e'er sink so low,
That you should fear such foes to face,
   Forgetful of the Alamo?
Or offer, coward like, to pay
   Five millions for your conquered right?
Rouse, rouse your minds without delay.
   Up, men of Texas, to the fight!

Ye strove before in honored time,
   And well your rifles told the tale,
Will Texans now yield up their clime,
   Or let their noble courage fail?
Remember well the Alamo;
   And let the name your souls unite
To deal destruction on the foe.
   Up, men of Texas, to the fight!

Arouse! arouse! your flag's unfurled;
   Seek victory or win your graves.
Show proudly forth to all the world,
   That Texians never can be slaves.
Oh! let the memory of the past
   To noble deeds your souls incite;
Be firm, be valiant to the last.
   Up, men of Texas, to the fight!

Discussion

1. What was the occasion of these lines?
2. Explain as many as you can of the references in this poem to events in Texas history.

An Awful Christmas Morning
by Governor J. W. Throckmorton, 1842

*The scene of this adventure is near the present town of
McKinney. It is a typical frontier experience.*

In December, 1842, Wesley Clements, Sam Young,
and a Mr. Whistler, with their families, made a settlement on Honey Creek, seven or eight miles north
west of the Throckmorton neighborhood (near the
present town of McKinney). After the construction of
one cabin, Young returned to the old home for provisions.

On Christmas morning the two men went to work
not very far from the house to cut logs for another
cabin. It seems that the Indians had discovered them
and were ambushed, ready to attack them. Whistler
was shot down and instantly killed. Clements escaped
and got within forty or fifty yards of the cabin, when
he was confronted by two Indians who had crept up
to attack the women and children. While still engaged
with these Indians in a hand-to-hand conflict the pursuing party arrived and cleft his head with a hatchet.

His wife had started to his assistance with a rifle
when he fell. She returned to the house pursued by
the Indians. On her entrance Mrs. Young closed the
door, and Mrs. Clements presented the gun at the
Indians through the crevices between the logs. From
this cause, or fearing that help might be near at hand

240

the Indians, after scalping the dead man, quickly disappeared.

Before the attack was made, Mrs. Whistler had gone to the spring for water. As soon as she heard the shooting and the screams of the women, she knew it was an attack. She did not doubt that all were killed; and jumped in the branch, so that the Indians could not trail her footprints, and followed it to the creek. There she found that the backwater from the creek had formed a drift of wood. At that moment she heard a bell coming towards her, and, realizing that the Indians were in pursuit of the animal wearing it, she hastily hid herself beneath the drift, with only her head above the water. She saw the Indians catch her husband's mare not twenty yards away.

Hearing no other noise, and still fearing she might be pursued, she attempted to follow the bed of the creek in order to make her escape. But the waters were too deep, and she was compelled to make her way through briers and dense thickets. Late in the evening she reached Throckmorton's settlement, entirely destitute of clothing, and bleeding from hundreds of wounds on her person, made by thorns and brush in her wild and reckless efforts to get through them.

The other two women remained in the house some time after the attack, and then took their children, a gun, and an axe, and followed the road made by their party in going to the place. At the creek they met two men camped on the banks of the stream. These men brought them in their wagon to the settlement. There, to the surprise of all three, the unfortunate women met.

The next morning seven men only could be spared to go after the remains of the dead men and the household effects of their families. They brought the bodies and buried them near the graves of Silkwood and Thompson, and thus was begun the first graveyard in Collin county. The coffins were hewn from slabs split from large trees.

Discussion

1. Compare this account with other stories of Indian massacres.
2. Tell how Mrs. Whistler escaped.
3. How were coffins made in the frontier settlements?

The Death of Flaco
by Sam Houston, 1843

Flaco was chief of the friendly Lipan Indians, and was some-times used by the Texans as a scout.

EXECUTIVE DEPARTMENT,
WASHINGTON, March 28, 1843.

To the Lipans.

MY BROTHERS: My heart is sad. A dark cloud rests upon your nation. Grief has sounded in your camp. The voice of Flaco is silent. His words are not heard in council. The chief is no more. His life has fled to the Great Spirit. His eyes are closed. His heart no longer leaps at the sight of the buffalo!

The voices of your camp are no longer heard to cry, "Flaco has returned from the chase!" Your chiefs look down on the earth and groan in trouble. Your warriors weep. The loud voice of grief is heard from your women and children. The song of birds is silent. The ear of your people hears no pleasant sound. Sorrow whispers in the winds. The noise of the tempest passes—it is not heard. Your hearts are heavy.

The name of Flaco brought joy to all hearts. Joy was on every face! Your people were happy. Flaco is no longer seen in the fight; his voice is no longer heard in battle; the enemy no longer make a path for his glory; his valor is no longer a guard for your people; the right arm of your nation is broken. Flaco was a friend

243

to his white brothers. They will not forget him. They will remember the red warrior.

His father will not be forgotten. We will be kind to the Lipans. Grass shall not grow in the path between us. Let your wise men give the council of peace. Let your young men walk in the white path. The gray-headed men of your nation will teach wisdom. I will hold my red brothers by the hand.

Thy brother,
SAM HOUSTON.

Discussion

1. Who was Flaco?

2. How did General Houston learn to write in Indian style?

3. What does he urge the Lipans to do?

4. What promise does he make them?

Drawing the Black Beans
by Thomas Jefferson Green, 1843

After the Santa Fe Expedition, the Mexicans made several raids into Texas. At this Texans were angered, and President Houston called for volunteers to invade and punish Mexico. General Somervell, who led the troops, went as far as the Rio Grande, and then turned back. About three hundred of his men, however, refused to give up the raid. They chose Colonel Fisher for their leader and pushed on to Mier, a town in Mexico. Here, on the day after Christmas, 1842, a battle was fought with two thousand Mexicans. The Texans, though they did not know it at the time, had almost won the day when they, themselves, surrendered and were marched as prisoners toward Mexico City. When they reached Salado they mutinied and escaped, but after nearly starving in the mountains, they were recaptured, taken back to Salado, the scene of their mutiny, and one-tenth of them were shot. The rest were taken to Mexico and imprisoned in the castle of Perote. General Green, who tells the following story, was one of the prisoners who was so fortunate as to draw a white bean and escape a sad fate.

245

Soon after they arrived, our men received the melancholy intelligence that they were to be decimated, and each tenth man shot.

It was now too late to resist this horrible order. Our men were closely ironed and drawn up in front of all their guards, who were in readiness to fire. Could they have known it previously, they would have again charged their guards, and made them pay dearly for this last breach of faith. It was now too late! A manly gloom and a proud defiance filled all faces. They had but one resort, and that was to invoke their country's vengeance upon their murderers, consign their souls to God, and die like men.

The decimator, Colonel Domingo Huerta, who was especially nominated to this black deed, had arrived at Salado ahead of our men. The "Red cap" company were to be the executioners; those men whose lives had been so humanely spared by our men at this place on the 11th of February.

The decimation took place by the drawing of black and white beans from a small earthen mug. The white ones signified life, and the black death. One hundred and fifty-nine white beans were placed in the bottom of the mug with seventeen black ones upon the top of them. The beans were not stirred, and had so slight a shake that it was perfectly clear that they had not been mixed together. Such was their anxiety to execute Captain Cameron, and perhaps the balance of the officers, that first Cameron, and afterward the other officers, were made to draw a bean each from the mug in this condition.

Cameron said, with his usual coolness, "Well, boys, we have to draw, let's be at it;" so saying, he thrust his hand into the mug, and drew out a white bean. Next came Colonel Wilson, who was chained to him; then Captain Ryan, and then Judge Gibson, all of whom drew white beans. Next came Captain Eastland, who drew the first black one, and then came the balance of the men. The knocking off the irons from the unfortunates alone told who they were.

They all drew their beans with that manly dignity and firmness which showed them superior to their condition. None showed change of countenance; and as the black beans failed to depress so did the white beans fail to elate. Some of lighter temper jested over the tragedy. One would say: "Boys, this beats raffling all to pieces;" another would say: "This is the tallest gambling scrape I ever was in."

Major Cocke, when he first drew the fatal bean, held it up before his forefinger and thumb, and with a smile of contempt said: "Boys, I told you so; I never failed in my life to draw a prize."

Soon after, the fated men were placed in a separate courtyard, where about dark they were executed. Several of our men were permitted to visit the unfortunates to receive their dying requests.

Just previous to the firing they were bound together with cords, and their eyes being bandaged they were set upon a log near the wall with their backs to the executioners. They all begged the officer to shoot them in front and at a short distance. This he refused; and, to make his cruelty as refined as possible, he fired at several paces.

During the martyrdom of these patriots the main body of our men were separated from them by a stone wall some fifteen feet high. The next morning, as they marched on the road to Mexico, they passed the bodies of their dead comrades, whose bones now lie upon the plains of Salado, a perishing remembrance of exalted patriotism.

Texans in a Mexican Prison
by Thomas Jefferson Green, 1843

General Green's story is here resumed where the prisoners reached Perote.

Upon our arrival at the village of Perote, in looking north about one mile we could see the massive walls of the castle, with its numerous port-holes and dark-mouthed artillery. Upon nearer approach, in making our way through its winding entrance, and across the drawbridge over the great moat, the din of arms and the clank of chains opened our eyes to the reality of imprisonment.

There is a mockery in many things in Mexico, and now there was a mock mercy by way of three days' grace extended to us before our chains were riveted. During these three days we had the privilege of walking about in certain parts of the castle in the daytime, estimating its capacity, military strength, etc.

At 9 o'clock of the fourth day after our confinement the Mier men were ordered to stand aside to receive their chains, a full ton of which had been brought out and laid in a heap, with a corresponding quantity of cumbrous, rudely made clevises to fit around the ankles. Here stood the fat old officer in charge, a Captain Gozeman. He desired Fisher and me to make choice of our chains. In fact there was no choice between them, the lightest weighing about twenty pounds; and even if there had been any difference, neither of us was in the temper to make the choice. We held forth our feet, the one a right, and the other a left foot, and the son of Vulcan riveted us together as though we had been a pair of unbroken oxen just being introduced to the yoke.

Colonel Fisher and I being first ironed, laughed at the "jewelry," as the boys called the chains. We started to our cells, but the inconvenience of being coupled so closely together determined us to separate. Upon reaching our cell, we looked out for the means of breaking so large a chain. Texians are a most ingenious people, and are usually equal to the emergency. We soon found means to accomplish our purpose.

In our prison room lay a loose stone, about one foot across, one side of which was slightly concave. In the room we also found a six-pound cannon shot. We sat flat upon the floor with the stone in our laps, the concave side up, and covered with a blanket as a non-conductor of sound, to prevent the alarm of the sentinel at the door. Then, placing the middle link of the chain across the concave surface of the stone, and another fold of the blanket over the link, we commenced hammering upon it until it came to fit the stone, turning it over and beating it back until it also fitted the other side, and thus, after twenty turnings of the link it parted, leaving each of us about five feet of chain.

Our companions in turn were all ironed, and many were the devices they resorted to in order to free themselves from their chains when not in the presence of the officers. In that horribly cold place, sleeping upon the cold pavement, with the still colder iron for your bedfellow, is no pleasant situation. Some would bribe the blacksmith to make them leaden instead of iron rivets, which, when blackened with charcoal, had much the appearance of iron, while they could be easily taken out or reheaded. One medio (half a dollar) would buy a leaden rivet; and for some time this ruse was practiced. Our old friend told the governor that it would require as many blacksmiths to keep us ironed as there were Texians in the castle.

Our rations were such as, even without labor, would hardly have kept soul and body together. We fortunately had a small balance of funds. So long as it lasted, our room-mates made out pretty well. A medio each of lard, onions, and red pepper, cut fine, put into our rations of poor beef, and re-cooked over a small earthen stove, made quite a savory meal for several. We also purchased sugar and coffee, and every day, at 12 o'clock, from the milkman, a gallon of leche de burra, donkey's milk. When we had the means, all of us took a hand at cooking.

A short time after we were ironed, our fat friend very politely informed us that we must prepare to go to work. We very politely replied that, as we were Texian officers, we would do no such thing. He went with our reply to the governor. April 6th our corpulent friend returned to our prison and said that he had positive orders from the governor to make us go to work. Colonel Fisher, Captain Reese, and Lieutenant Clarke, the only Mier officers present, pledged themselves to me that they would be shot down sooner than submit to the order, and so we informed him.

Time passed heavily, and though we were repeatedly told that we must go to work, yet the order was not enforced. The balance of the men, with the exception of those who had been excused, from inability or other causes, were, however, compelled to work.

The anniversary of the Texians' triumph over Santa Anna at San Jacinto found my finances reduced to the last extremity. Was that day to be passed in silence? No! And though I might have never expected to own another ounce, we would have rejoiced in our country's triumph. So that last doubloon was devoted to our country's jubilee. We bought seven gallons of "vino mescal," as many of donkey's milk, thirty dozen eggs, a large loaf of sugar, and used all our cooking utensils and water jars in the mixing of egg-nog; and such egg-nog as never before was seen or drunk under the nineteenth degree of north latitude!

We went around to the prison rooms and summoned all hands to attend the thanksgiving. When those noble fellows stood round the bowl in rags, with their "jewelry" riveted upon their ankles, brought up and tied around the waist with a cord, the sight filled my heart to overflowing. Though the body was oppressed, they looked like caged lions, and every face bespoke the invincible spirit of a free man.

251

Discussion

1. How were the Texans treated in the castle of Perote?
2. Describe the prison.
3. How did the prisoners celebrate San Jacinto Day?

The Escape from Perote
by Thomas Jefferson Green, 1843

I determined to return to my country or perish in the attempt. To escape from this strong place, guarded as it was with the most unremitting vigilance, was considered impossible by the Mexicans, and the project required the greatest caution, coolness and calculation. I made known my determination to Captain Reese, who agreed to join me in the enterprise, and also to stake his life upon the issue.

Our first plan was to scale the different walls, the height of which we could carefully estimate by the eye, during some stormy night when the sentinels could be most easily passed. We accordingly set about making arrangements. With all arrangements completed for our migration we were yet prevented from so doing at this time, account of the following circumstances:

In the central one of our prison rooms, which contained thirty-six of our countrymen, a few lion hearted fellows determined also to make the attempt at escaping. They had commenced digging through an eight-foot wall, and if Captain Reese and I escaped by scaling the walls, which we now considered pretty certain of accomplishing, it would break up all further chances of others doing so by any means whatever. We then determined to join the plan of going through the walls, and all escaping at the same time.

All who determined upon the hazard were in high spirits, when we were informed, through General

Thompson, that we would be released on the 13th of
June, Santa Anna's birthday. The 13th of June drew
near, and every officer we met told us that "in a little time we would leave that place and return to our
country and friends." The soldiers, by way of congrat-
ulating us, in their mixture of Spanish and English,
would make a flourish peculiar to the Mexican people,
dash their right hand through their left in the direction of Texas, and say, "Poco tiempo Texas" (Texas in
a little while). Even this from the most stupid soldier
flattered our desire; but the 13th came and went, and
no liberation. The next day it was promised, but the
next failed of liberation. The next, and still the next,
came and passed under a like promise from our officers, bringing with each successive day the chagrin of
disappointment to take the place of joyous hopes.

Our arched cells were twenty feet wide by seventy
long, with a door at one end opening in the castle,
and a loophole at the other opening upon the outside,
underneath which is the great moat. This loophole
is a small aperture, upon the outside about four by
twelve inches, and gradually widening through the
eight-foot wall to about two feet upon the inside.

The tools with which we worked were narrow, in-
ferior carpenter's chisels. Some of our men were employed in the carpenter shop making artillery carriages; and as they would come to their meals, and sleep
in the same prison cells, they would smuggle the chisels out of the shop under their blankets.

As a water-drip will wear away the hardest granite,
so the breach in the wall gradually grew deeper under
our incessant labor. This work was principally accom-

plished by drilling holes into the stone and mortar with the chisel, and prying off small pieces; and frequently, after a hard day's labor, not more than a hatful could be loosed. On the first day of July the hole had been drilled down to a thin shell on the outer side, which could be easily burst out, after the final preparation was made for leaving.

For some weeks previous to our escape, those who intended to go were busily engaged, every safe opportunity, in completing their arrangements—fixing their knapsacks, saving all the bread they could procure, laying aside every cent to purchase fat bacon and chocolate. Having been furnished money by a friend in Mexico, I was enabled to supply several with sugar, coffee, and bacon.

At length, Sunday, the second day of July, opened upon us with a favorable sign. We passed the word for all who intended to go to be in readiness by night. Sixteen of our number finally determined to make the effort.

At seven o'clock we commenced our final preparations before leaving the room. This was to remove the shell of the wall yet upon the outside, then to make one end of the rope fast inside of the room, and pass it through. By this we would have to let ourselves down to the bottom of the moat. When this was done, it was found that the hole was too small upon the outside to allow any but the smallest of our men to pass through, and it required two hours hard work to scale some pieces of stone and mortar from one side of it, so as to permit the larger ones to pass. This required until nine o'clock.

All things being now ready, John Toowig, a gallant son of the Emerald Isle, got into the hole feet foremost, and, drawing his bundle after him, inch by inch squeezed out, and let himself down hand over hand about thirty feet to the bottom of the moat. The depth and smallness of the hole rendered this operation exceedingly slow. Another and another followed, and at half past twelve, after three hours and a half of hard labor, all of the sixteen had safely landed.

The moon had gone down at eight o'clock, and, being favored by the darkness in the bottom of the moat through which the sentinels overhead could not penetrate, we slowly crossed over to the outer wall in Indian file, then felt along the wall until we came to a flight of narrow steps eighteen inches wide, up which we crawled upon all fours. When we reached the top we breathed more freely, for we were now in the wide world, and felt more like free men; and as the sentinels drolled out their sleepy notes of "centinela alerta" (sentinel, watch out), we jumped up, and cracked our heels together three times, as a substitute for cheers three times three.

255

Discussion

1. How did General Green first plan to escape from the castle?
2. Why did he abandon this plan?
3. How did the Texans finally escape?
4. Describe the preparations that they were making for several days before the escape?
5. What finally became of those who remained in the prison?

Indian "Talks"
by Pa-ha-you-co and Roasting-Ear, 1845

*Pa-ha-you-co was a Comanche chief. These "talks" were
dictated by the Indians in their own tongue to an interpreter who translated them and sent them to President
Anson Jones.*

Trading House, January 19, 1845.

PA-HA-YOU-CO'S TALK

Be good to Brothers: Never give up your efforts to
make peace with your Red Brothers. Whenever any of
them come to see you, smoke the pipe of peace with
them and give them good talk before they leave. If
you do that, everybody will know you are appointed
by the great chief, and they will come to you to make
peace. And you must give them presents when they
come. That will not hurt you, but if they should cut
your meat off, that would hurt you.

The reason I came here was to bring the white prisoner and deliver him up to you. I know his people are
anxious about him. I do not keep my words hid nor
tell lies, but what I say is true. I am anxious and so are
all my tribe to make peace, and what I say now I will
stick to as long as I live.

My people are now gone to the Spanish country
(Mexico) for foolishness, and when they get their fill
of foolishness they will come back here.

256

When Colonel Eldridge told me that Texas wished to make peace with me, I was glad. I listened to his talk good. And I have told Buffalo Hump that he must not forget what he heard at the last council, but hold fast to it and never give it up.

When I was a young man we were accustomed to go among the white people and trade. I am anxious that that time should return. We wish to be at peace with all, and raise our children at peace. My war chief, The-Bear-With-a-Short-Tail, is brave, but he prefers peace to war. He has come to see that peace is good. He is next war chief to Buffalo Hump. Now we love our White brethren the same as Our Red brothers.

When my brother came back from the council we were all glad to hear his words, for they were good. All the other tribes of Indians know me, and know that I wish for peace with all. You that are listening to me may think that I am telling lies, but the Great Spirit who looks upon me now knows that I speak truth.

Whenever any of my men or chiefs come in to see you, you must give them presents so that when they return home the people may see that the whites are friendly. The Spaniards when they send for us to make peace, steal our horses; but we believe that what the white people tell us is true.

The Buffaloes are close by here, and we are obliged to come down with our families among them. All tribes and nations have some bad men who will steal, but none but my good men shall come, and we will do our best to keep all from stealing.

In the spring some of my men will be down about San Antonio, and they may wish to go into the settle-

257

ments. If they do, they will come with a white flag, so that the whites may know they are friendly and not hurt them. We shall range from the Colorado to the Guadalupe, and we wish to be friendly.

I mention this so that they may know that we will be there hunting, and not to steal. The Witchitas are like dogs. They will steal. You may feed a dog well at night, and he will steal all your meat before morning. This is the way with the Witchitas.

This is all I have to say. If you listen to my talk, I shall be glad, and everything will be good.

ROASTING-EAR'S TALK

I have listened to Pa-ha-you-co's talk, and it is good. I am glad to hear it, and believe he speaks truth. I have listened to him twice now, and his talk is the same. He wishes to be at peace with the Whites and I hope peace will be effected.

I have been listening to white men since I was a boy, and now I am gray-headed. They have told me some lies, but I believe what they say now is true. What we say in the presence of the Great Spirit we must stick to. We cannot lie when we call him to witness what we say, but must speak truth. We love the white men, women, and children the same as our own, and it should be our desire to make peace with all for the sake of our women and children if nothing else. I will do my best to make peace between the Whites and all the Red men.

I am glad to find that my friend here is disposed for peace, and hope you will satisfy him before he goes back. This is all I have to say.

Discussion

1. How did the Comanches show their friendship for visitors?
2. Who was meant by "the great chief"?
3. What business brought the Indians near the white settlements?
4. Where in Texas did the buffalo range in 1845?
5. Where was this talk made?

Farewell to the Republic
by President Anson Jones, 1846

An Austin newspaper thus described the effect of President Jones's farewell address upon his audience:

> *The President arose and delivered his valedictory. He was loudly applauded. During the whole time the most intense emotion thrilled every bosom—tears crept unconsciously from the eye of many a weather-beaten Texan, who had toiled and suffered and bled to establish an independent government—to win freedom for a people who were now being stricken from the roll of nations; they seemed to feel as if the Republic of Texas was indeed "no more."*

260

*Gentlemen of the Senate and of
the House of Representatives:*

The great measure of annexation, so earnestly desired by the people of Texas, is happily consummated. The present occasion, so full of interest to us and to all the people of this country, is an earnest of that consummation, and I am happy to tender to you my cordial congratulations on an event the most extraordinary in the annals of the world.

A government is changed both in its officers and its law; not by violence and disorder, but by the deliberate and free consent of its citizens.

The lone star of Texas, which ten years since arose amid clouds, over fields of carnage, and obscurely shone for a while, has culminated, has passed on and become fixed forever in that glorious constellation which all free men and lovers of freedom in the world must reverence and adore—the American Union. Blending its rays with its sister stars, long may it continue to shine, and may a gracious Heaven smile upon this consummation of the wishes of the two Republics now joined together in one. "May the Union be perpetual, and may it be the means of conferring benefits and blessings upon the people of all the States," is my ardent prayer. The final act in this great drama is now performed. The Republic of Texas is no more.

PART SIX
The State

The Ranger's Song
by James T. Lytle

The famous Texas Rangers were organized as early as the beginning of the Revolution to protect the frontiers from Indian attacks, and the organization has continued ever since. The Rangers have frequently done heroic service fighting Indians and repelling Mexican invasions. Their duties often, in times past, led them into exploits as romantic as they were dangerous. It is sometimes said that the Rangers were first organized during the Republic. This is a mistake.

Mount! mount! and away o'er the green prairie wide;
The sword is our scepter, the fleet steed our pride.
Up! up! with our flag, let its bright star gleam out:
Mount! mount! and away on the wild border-scout!

We care not for danger, we heed not the foe;
Where our brave steeds can bear us, right onward we go,
And never, as cowards, can we fly from the fight,
While our belts bear a blade, our star sheds its light.

Then mount and away! give the fleet steed the rein;
The Ranger's at home on the prairies again.
Spur! spur in the chase, dash on to the fight,
Cry vengeance for Texas! and God speed the right.

The might of the foe gathers thick on our way;
They hear our wild shout as we rush to the fray.
What to us is the fear of the death-stricken plain?
We have braved it before, and will brave it again.

The death-dealing bullets around us may fall,
They may strike, they may kill, but they cannot appal;
Through the red field of carnage right onward we'll wade,
While our guns carry ball, and our hands wield the blade.

Hurrah, my brave boys! ye may fare as ye please,
No Mexican banner now floats in the breeze
'Tis the flag of Columbia that waves o'er each height,
While on its proud folds our star sheds its light.

Then mount and away! give the fleet steed the rein;
The Ranger's at home on the prairies again.
Spur! spur in the chase, dash on to the fight,
Cry vengeance for Texas! and God speed the right.

The Texans at Monterey
by Samuel C. Reid, 1846

One of the first important events in the history of Texas after she joined the United States was the Mexican War. In this contest the Texas Rangers, under Colonel John Coffee "Jack" Hays, played an important part. Captain Reid here tells of their share in the capture of Monterey, an event of which he was a personal witness.

As soon as news of the critical situation of the American army on the Rio Grande reached Texas, and General Taylor's call for volunteers was heard throughout the new State, the spirit of patriotism burst forth anew to gleam as brightly as in the days of its infant liberty.

On the western frontier, that portion of the state nearest the seat of war, preparations for the campaign were most active and most earnest. There was wiping of rifles and molding of bullets, cleaning of pistols and grinding of knives, packing of wallets and saddling of steeds. Every step of preparation was made amid the encouraging smiles of mothers, wives, and sisters, who cheerfully came forth to lend their aid, making wallets and molding leaden messengers of death.

In thirty-six hours after the express arrived, Capt. Ben McCulloch had raised a choice company on the banks of the Guadalupe, and set out for the seat of hostilities. This company was perhaps the best mounted, armed, and equipped corps that was out in the ranging service.

The middle of September found the American army at Monterey, preparing for its capture. Independence Hill, between seven and eight hundred feet high, is not only the most inaccessible height, but also the most important. It commands the western approaches to the Bishop's Palace, and thus forms a key to the entrance of Monterey on its western side. The height was defended by a piece of artillery, and during the night a large reinforcement had been thrown forward from the Bishop's Palace. Here they remained, as they supposed, in perfect security.

At three o'clock, on the morning of the 22d, the troops that had been detailed to storm the fort on Independence Hill were aroused from their slumbers. It was dark and cloudy, with a heavy, thick mist. The command consisted of three companies of artillery, under Captain Vinton, three companies of infantry, under Captain Screven, and seven companies of the Texas Rangers, under Colonel Hays and Lieutenant-Colonel Walker. The whole force, numbering four hundred and sixty-five men besides the officers, was under Lieutenant-Colonel Childs, who had been assigned to lead this storming party.

The expedition was looked upon as a forlorn hope, but not a word was spoken, save by the officers in a low tone, as they marshaled their men in the darkness of night. The solemn stillness that prevailed indicated the firm purpose in the minds of the men.

The short, quick word of command, "forward," was given, and the column wound its way by a right flank along the dark road, passing through a cornfield, until it arrived at the base of the hill. Now commenced the ascent, which at a distance had appeared sufficiently difficult, and when actually grappled with, required all the vigor and strength of the most hardy.

Forward pressed the men, invigorated by the fresh morning air, until they arrived within a hundred yards of the crest of the hill. A crash of musketry from the enemy's skirmishers announced that they were discovered. An incessant random fire was poured down upon the stormers, but not a shot was returned—not a word uttered.

The two columns steadily advanced, climbing over projecting crags by means of the fissures in the rocks, or clinging to the stunted, thorny bushes, until within about twenty yards of the top, when a shout and yell rose on the air, amid the rattling of musketry from the regulars and the whistling of the rifle balls of the Texians. The enemy were appalled, and driven back from the brow of the slope. Then came the deadly struggle. Panting and breathless, men and officers strove to gain the height, contending with the rocky steep as well as with the enemy. Peal after peal, and shout and cry, rang wildly forth for victory. Onward they rushed, braving the storm of hail, until they gained the brow, and with a loud huzza bore back the foe, while the mist now left the mountain top for the sunbeam's warmer glow to shine upon the triumphant colors of our victorious troops.

The Mexicans fled in confusion, some towards the Palace, others headlong down the hill. They succeeded, however, in carrying off a piece of cannon, our men being too much exhausted to pursue them farther. The loss of the enemy was considerable, while on our part, though it was but few in numbers, some of our noblest spirits fell.

But the critical moment was still to come. Large reinforcements of cavalry and infantry were seen ascending the road from the city to the Bishop's Palace. Battalions of infantry formed in front of the Palace. Their crowded ranks and glistening bayonets presented a bold front. Squadrons of light horsemen with bright lances and fluttering flags, and heavy cavalry with scopets (escopeta, a type of short barreled shotgun) and broadswords gleaming in the sun, made a most imposing sight.

Their bugle notes now echoed forth the charge. Victory. Onward they came. Most bravely were they met. One volley from that long line, with a deadly fire from the Texians, made them reel and stagger back. Above the battle-cry was heard the hoarse command to "charge." On, on rushed our men, with shouts of triumph, driving the retreating enemy, horse and foot, down the ridge, past the Palace, and even to the bottom of the hill, into the streets of the city. The victory was won—the Palace ours.

Discussion

1. What were the causes of the Mexican War?
2. Who were the Rangers?
3. Describe their preparations for going to the war.
4. Write a short account of the assault on the Bishop's Palace.

A Ranger's Story
by Captain George C. Hendricks

In the fifties Captain George C. Hendricks was a famous Ranger and Indian fighter. He led a life full of dash and excitement, and is said to have narrowly escaped death many times by tomahawk or Indian rifle. The following story which he tells illustrates the valuable services the Rangers frequently performed for Texas.

We were professional rangers, serving sometimes under Ben McCulloch and sometimes under Jack Hays. We had been scouting on the headwaters of the Rio Pecos, when news reached us that the Comanches were making fearful depredations all along the western tributaries of the Colorado River, and that unless we could furnish immediate help, the settlements west of the Colorado would have to be abandoned.

On receipt of this news about thirty of us were dispatched to the relief of the frontier settlers. As Hays was perfectly familiar with all the border settlements, he suggested that we should go at once to the Enchanted Hill (Enchanted Rock, between Fredericksburg and Llano) and make that point the base of our operations. It was a good place for intercepting Indians on their raids.

Three friendly Indians were detailed to go with us. One of them was a Comanche who had been wounded and captured in a fight with Ben McCulloch's rangers and then carried to a hospital, where he was treated, nursed, and cured by the kindness of Texas women. He was reclaimed from barbarism and afterward became a valuable aid to McCulloch in trailing the savages. The other two were Cherokees who had joined the rangers under Hays.

We had camped in sight of the Enchanted Hill, when a 14-year-old boy, without hat or shoes, came dashing into our midst about sunrise, his horse's hoofs striking fire from the rocky trail along which he was riding. He brought the startling news that a family had been murdered by the Indians and that our assistance was wanted badly and at once.

The shrill notes of the bugle put us into our saddles. Pressing the spurs close to our horses' sides, we sped away with clattering hoofs to the scene of the massacre. In a little while we were on the spot and found the boy's story too true. Two children were lying dead, their skulls crushed in with a murderous tomahawk. The father was lying near with two ugly gunshot wounds in his body. A 17-year-old girl had been carried away captive, while the mother seemed bereft of her reason. She would not consent for us to remain long enough to bury the dead, but cried wildly: "My daughter, oh, my poor daughter, rescue her; rescue her or I shall die."

We left two of our men to bury the children and comfort the grief-stricken mother, and, with our Indians as guides, we dashed away on the trail of the savages. Within an hour and a half our scouts sighted the hostiles, in camp about two miles below a bluff. They had sent out a hunting party, which would diminish their fighting strength, and now was the time to strike and whip them in detail.

A brisk ride of fifteen or twenty minutes brought us in sight of their camp. They were evidently barbecuing fresh meat; but we were five hundred yards away and wanted a nearer and better view. We found a ravine running in the right direction. A thick, scrubby undergrowth that fringed its banks enabled us to approach to within about two hundred yards of their camp fires.

Here we had as full and complete a view as we could have desired, but at this critical juncture two Indian dogs came chasing a mule-eared rabbit right into the midst of our party. The dogs, discovering the white intruders, drew their tails between their legs, and with ears dropped and hair turned the wrong way, gave a warning yelp and made for the Indian camp as fast as their feet could carry them. As no time was to be lost our captain gave us a few words of instruction.

"Now, boys," he said, "some of us must spill a little blood; but keep perfectly cool and show your usual pluck and I do not fear the result." As we emerged from the thicket in a helter skelter charge we saw a great commotion in the Indian camp. So sudden and unexpected was our attack that one-half the Indians could not find their guns, and those who did had their nerves so completely unstrung that they did very poor shooting.

We rode straight into their camp and closed on them with our six-shooters, but most of them were in full flight across the open space between the camp and the river. The water being shallow they forded it with ease. Several of them, however, having their guns in easy reach, availed themselves of trees and logs and made a slow and stubborn retreat. As we drove the last of them into the river we paused to take a survey of the situation.

We found that two of our number had been killed and five wounded, and five Indians lay dead on the ground. But now a startling discovery was made. The captive girl was missing. Where could she be? No one could remember seeing her as we charged the camp, nor did anyone see her in the running fight between the camp and the river. There was now greater excitement among us than there had been during the hottest of the fight.

"Boys," said our captain, "there has been foul play somewhere. We will find that girl or remain on the warpath until we die with old age." A few moments more and the mystery was solved. She was found just outside the battleground in a dying condition. We raised her tenderly from a pool of blood. There was a feeble movement of her slender arms, a twitching of her girlish lips, a quivering of her frail form, a beseeching expression in her beautiful brown eyes, and her soul flew away to the presence of her God.

When the Indians saw that they were whipped, they had undertaken to carry their captive with them in their flight, but seeing that they must inevitably be overtaken, they resolved to murder her rather than have her restored to her mother and friends. She was pierced by three rifle balls, one passing through the region of the heart.

After a short consultation held amid sighs and sobs, it was decided to carry her remains to the great bluff and bury her on the loftiest peak of the precipice,

272

where an endless view of the landscape could be had, and where the gurgling waters of the Llano, glistening and sparkling in the sunlight far, far below, could chant her requiem through all coming time.

Who should break the sad news to the disconsolate and heart-broken mother, waiting, longing for the returning notes of the rangers' bugle?

Discussion

1. Tell what services the Rangers performed for the frontier settlements.
2. Who sometimes acted as scouts and guides for the Rangers?
3. Write a description of this battle with the Indians.
4. Why did the Indians want to keep this girl a prisoner?

A Bear Story
by Frederick Law Olmsted, 1857

The writer of this story was a noted traveler from New York, who just before the Civil War made a tour of the southern States. The bear story is without doubt an exaggeration, but it may have historical value as an example of the accounts with which the frontiersmen regaled the "tenderfoot." (Olmsted went on to become the premier landscape architect of his day, designing Central Park in New York City.)

While in the mountains the settlers told us with fresh excitement, the story of a great bear hunt which had but recently come off. The hero was one of the German hermits, named P____, a famous sportsman. Not long before the hunt he had had a personal difficulty with a bear. After the animal had drawn his fire he closed with the hunter, now armed only with a knife, upon a rocky ledge, and attempted either to throw him over the precipice, or to force him, in pure vengeance, to roll down the steep with himself. Almost crushed with the hug, P____ , with his one free hand, succeeded in giving the bear seven deep stabs, and left him dead upon the verge.

On the last occasion he had wounded a bear, which took to its heels and disappeared in a pile of rocks. Following with all of his speed, P____ found a hole down which the bear seemed to have dropped. Convinced that his shot had been fatal, yet unable to enter the cavity, he pried a large stone over the mouth, and went for assistance. His hut-companion returned with him, and they at first attempted to smoke the bear out. Not succeeding in this, they battered the edge of the hole till it was large enough to enter.

Then, held by the heels, P____ went in on his hands and knees in search of his booty. After some not very pleasant groping, he found the carcass, and, attaching a rope, it was hauled out, a magnificent bear, worth a good deal in cash and much more in glory.

But while half smothered in the cave, the hunter had heard, at no great distance, an indistinct growl, which indicated that more fun was to be had if properly applied for. It was a hazardous experiment, but one that exactly suited P___'s humor, to enter and have a hand to hand fight in the dark with the growler, whoever he was.

Arming himself with a freshly capped and cocked pistol and placing a knife between his teeth, he crept cautiously in again. The passage shortly became narrow, and he soon reached a turn which he could only pass feet foremost. Retreating a bit he turned himself and pushed on. After clearing the obstacle he found himself free, and heard, now close before him, the steady breathing of a bear. It was as dark as Erebus, but hit or miss he resolved to have a shot. Aiming deliberately at the sound, he fired two barrels, then took himself out as fast as hands and knees would carry him. But no stir followed, and it was impossible to tell the result.

Piling the rocks again over the aperture, the two returned to their hut, manufactured torches of wax from a bee tree, and calling a neighbor or two to see the sport, went again to the den. Armed now with a torch, P____ forced himself to where he had been before, and saw his bear lying dead. It was dragged out.

After a congratulatory and recuperative draught of whisky all round, P____ resolved on further explorations. He found, beyond the scene of his last adventure, a narrow cleft in the rocks. He had hardly squeezed himself into this, when he suddenly found his hand in contact with a third bear—dead. It had probably been smothered by their smoke. This, too, was got out amid an excitement that made the woods ring with echoes.

But if three bears had been found, that was no reason why there should not be more beyond. Creeping down again to the cleft, he squeezed in, head foremost, as before. He had not progressed far when he was met with a savage roar, and the glare of a pair of mad eyes in motion directly before him. He attempted to fall back, to recover himself, but one of the neighbors, who had made up his mind to have a finger in the pie, was close behind, and prevented, by his entangled body, any quick retreat; so aiming hurriedly between the eyes, P____ fired.

Before his excited senses had recovered from the reverberated din and smoke, he saw the eyes again in a different place, this time fixed in a steady gaze. He fired again. The echoes over, nothing more was to be seen or heard. Advancing cautiously once more, he came upon two warm carcasses, both shot between the eyes. Here was the end of the cave. He had killed the whole of the Bruin family.

Imagine the cheer when the five bears were carried by his neighbors, on poles, into the settlement, P____ striding modestly at the rear. A three days' feast of bear meat and whisky was proclaimed and celebrated, and P____, if he does not, like old Put (General Israel Putnam, famous for killing wolves in Connecticut under similar circumstances), find his way into history, will at least live long in local tradition.

An Anecdote of General Houston
Writer Unknown, 1860

*This story illustrates the democratic character of General Hous-
ton as well as the biting sarcasm which he could use when the
occasion required.*

It was the custom of General Houston, while governor, to mingle and talk with the people a good deal.

In 1860 he might have been seen almost daily on
Congress Avenue, Austin, Texas, standing at some
corner with a crowd around him. Upon one occasion,
and while in the center of a knot of men with whom
he was conversing in an animated manner, an individual, whom we will call Mr. K—, being determined to
get his ear, elbowed his way through the crowd, and,
suddenly confronting General Houston, addressed
him thus: "Governor, I am told you have devoted considerable attention to the culture of shrubbery. What
do you consider the best time for setting out shade
trees, and how?"

The general, being thus suddenly interrupted in the
middle of a sentence, lowered his shaggy eyebrows,
and quietly regarding his interlocutor a moment slowly replied, "The best time, Mr. K. is perhaps in the
winter, and the way in which I have succeeded best is
to set the roots down."

A shout went up, and Mr. K. went off.

278

Home Life During the Civil War
by Mrs. E. M. Loughery, 1861-65

This extract illustrates some of the hardships of the women during the war.

As soon as the tocsin of war sounded, nearly every man in the State capable of bearing arms enlisted and hurried to the front. After they had marched away sadness settled down over every home. Many business houses were closed, while the proprietors joined the army.

Our women were most worthy of such husbands, sons, and brothers. Here in Texas, as elsewhere in the South, the old fashioned spinning wheel, loom, and knitting needles were brought into requisition by our noble women, who worked busily through the days of storm that marked the war, and far into the nights, to supply the soldiers at the front and the dependent members of the family at home with needed clothing.

The ladies all over the State formed themselves into a sisterhood, to solicit contributions of clothing, provisions, and money for the relief of our soldiers. There were also committees formed for the relief of soldiers' families, many of whom were in utter destitution and would have actually suffered had not such action been taken. In many instances the mother and six or seven children were left without any resource, yet there were no cases of actual starvation.

279

The ladies never lost their ambition to appear well. The skill they displayed in making something out of nothing was really marvelous—and sometimes ridiculous. For stylish bonnets they made what were called skyscrapers. These were of enormous size, both in height and breadth, and were decked with a profusion of flowers. The ladies also made many beautiful hats and fans out of shucks and straw.

Notwithstanding the blockade of the coast, a few goods were brought into the country from Mexico, and daring blockade-runners occasionally brought supplies from Europe, but the greater part of what was needed was obtained by our own invention. For medicines, in many instances, we used barks, roots, and herbs, as the Indians do. For soda we burned corn cobs and used the ashes. For coffee there were various substitutes, such as parched sweet potatoes, rye, and okra-beans.

280

Dry goods were not to be had, except in very small quantities, and at fabulous prices. Calico of the best quality cost $50 a yard, Confederate money. Domestics and other goods were proportionately high. The negroes worked well during the war, and the farms supplied the country with provisions quite well.

These were hard times in Southern homes, but Southern women were as brave as Southern men. They met every hardship unfalteringly. They managed the slaves, while the men were fighting. They had the fields cultivated, and the crops grown and gathered. They had the cotton and the wool spun and woven into clothes. They fed the hungry, clothed the naked, housed the homeless, and nursed the sick.

Privation was nothing to them, so the Southern flag floated to the breeze.

Discussion

1. Describe the home life in Texas during the Civil War.
2. How did the people get most of their clothes and medicines?
3. What is meant by "running the blockade"?
4. How did the women help those who went to the war?
5. What is said of the faithfulness of the slaves?

A Yankee Soldier's Diary
1862

The Federal troops captured Galveston October 4, 1862, and held it until January 1, 1863, when the city was retaken by General Magruder. This diary was found after the battle on the body of a Union sergeant. It illustrates some of the conditions of the War.

After coming out of the cotton press, on the road to the other side of the island, we met the owner of the presses, and he asked that he might be allowed the privilege of removing his books, which was granted him. He also inquired whether we were to pay him for the use of his property, or calculated to take it. The commodore told him in very forcible terms that he intended to take it, the same as he would any other rebel property. After thanking him for the privilege of removing his books, the old Secesh (secessionist) left.

When our men came down from the city they brought with them many rebel relics, which they obtained in the stores while foraging: such as pipes, rebel buttons, inkstands, blacking, clocks, candlesticks, books, pails, brooms, and the like. We are in hopes, when the balance of the troops get here, business will revive, and everything look different from what it does at the present; and it needs a change here, for it is the most forsaken looking city that I ever saw.

To-night we have a Union man, a resident of the city with us, who has been obliged to quarter on board

the steamer *Harriet Lane*, and for whom they have offered $300, dead or alive. He seems to be very grate-
ful to us for the little hospitality we have shown him,
and although his house is in sight of our quarters, the
poor fellow is obliged to leave every night and quarter
on the wharf, away from his family. We that have our
folks securely at home and well provided for while we
are away, would think it much harder if we were right
in sight of our own houses, seeing our families literally starving before our eyes, and not able to get there.
The name of our Union friend is J. R. Romaine, and
he formerly resided in New York.

Saturday, December 27, 1862—Rose at reveille and
called the roll. Had breakfast, after which I went up
into the city with Lieutenant Newcomb, of Company
G, and visited several of the stores in the place, in
one of which I found a map of the State of Texas. We
found a store in which some stoves were stored, and I
then came down to the wharf and reported the same.
We broke open the store, and after taking what we
wanted, we concluded to make a reconnaissance in
the dwelling of a Secesh. We found there corn, beef,
furniture, and crockery, which we confiscated and
marched to the wharf. We were met by the Adjutant
and a guard, who told us to double-quick, as there
had been a raid of cavalry to the number of 75, who
had been endeavoring to cut us off. They had beat
the long roll and called the whole battalion to come
to our rescue. After supper we received orders to fall
in. We marched up into the city with two hundred
and twenty-five men, with rockets and blue lights to
signal the gunboats in case of attack. We scoured the

city all over, but found no rebel officers, as we had anticipated. In fact, I believe we did not see a single soul on the march. The only thing we did was to cut the telegraph wire, of which I saved a piece. We arrived at our quarters at about 12 o'clock at night, very tired with our day's and evening's tramp.

Some poor people came down today, and we gave them some of our hard-tack, for which they appeared very grateful. I got possession of two bank bills to day, in the safe of the store we entered, and one man got over $600 in Confederate notes.

Sunday, December 28—Rose at 6 o'clock, got breakfast and had orders to fall the men in for divine service at 10 o'clock. We did not have any, however, owing to the indisposition of the chaplain, or his laziness, I don't know which.

Wednesday, December 31—At 8:30 o'clock at night, while we were having a squad drill in the armory, the captain ordered me to detail twenty-five men, two sergeants, with myself, and make a scouting party, and we started up town with our handful of men to see what was going on. A dangerous piece of business it was, too, as the rebels could easily have cut us off and bagged every man of us. They are in the city to-night in considerable numbers, both cavalry and infantry.

We learned from a source on which we can rely that they intend burning the city tonight, and we saw, as we passed through the streets, lights burning in the houses at ten and half past ten, which is late to be up here. We also saw family carriages laden with household goods, ready for starting. Women were standing in the doors of the houses waiting for the time when the gunboats should retaliate, to leave. Others had bundles and were making for the other side of the island.

(The writer did not live to enter the balance of the history of his visit to Texas in his little book. He was killed this same night.)

Discussion

1. What was a "Secesh"?
2. Why did the soldiers not pay for what they took from the stores?
3. What kindnesses did they sometimes show the people of Galveston?

The Recapture of Galveston

GLORIOUS NEWS
GALVESTON RETAKEN

The Harriet Lane Captured
The Westfield Destroyed
600 Prisoners Taken

THE MOST BRILLIANT AFFAIR OF THE WAR

Galveston, Texas, January 1, 1863.

To S. Cooper, Adjutant-General.

This morning, the first of January, at 3 o'clock, I attacked the enemy's fleet and garrison at this place.

I captured the garrison and the steamer *Harriet Lane* and two barks and a schooner of the fleet.

The rest of the fleet, some four or five in number, and supplies. escaped ignominiously under cover of a flag of truce.

I have about six hundred prisoners and a large quantity of valuable stores, arms, etc. The *Harriet Lane* is very little injured. She was carried by boarding, from two high pressure cotton steamers manned by Texas cavalry and artillery.

The line troops were gallantly commanded by Col. Thomas Green, of Sibley's brigade, and the ships and artillery by Major Leon Smith, to whose energy and heroic daring the country is indebted for the successful execution of a plan which I had conceived for the destruction of the enemy's fleet. Col. Bagby, of Sibley's brigade, also commanded the volunteers from his regiment for the naval expedition, in which every officer and every man won for himself imperishable renown.

I am, sir, very respectfully your ob't serv't,

J. BANKHEAD MAGRUDER,
Maj. Gen. Com'd'g Dept., Dist. of Texas.

287

Discussion

1. How many vessels were captured by General Magruder in the Battle of Galveston?
2. How many prisoners did he capture?
3. How did he fortify the vessels that he used in the attack?
4. What does he say of the men who were under his command?

Federal Prisoners at Houston
1863

The article which follows appeared in the January 5, 1863 edition of the Houston Tri-Weekly Telegraph *newspaper.*

HOUSTON, January 2, 1863.

It having been given out that the Federal prisoners, captured in the recent battle at Galveston, would be up on the train this morning, a large concourse of citizens assembled at the depot, burning with curiosity to see the men who had come to desolate our land, but who had suddenly been brought up with a round turn by the unparalleled generalship of our noble commander. After waiting some two hours in the rain, the assemblage was gratified with the sound of the locomotive whistle, and presently the train came in view. It stopped about half a mile from the depot, where the Yankees were landed, formed into line, and under guard marched to the depot, and thence to their quarters, where they will remain for the present.

The colonel of the regiment, three captains, six lieutenants, and 350 non-commissioned officers, privates, and soldiers are all that could be brought on this train. The balance, some 275, will be sent up as soon as possible. Our reporter was kindly permitted by the officers in charge to pass the guard and mingle with the prisoners. From them he learned that the regiment had been in service only four months. They were mostly Americans; but an occasional foreigner might be seen among them, mostly Irish and Dutch.

Those with whom our reporter conversed were young men, and seemed very intelligent. They were all remarkably well dressed and accoutered, and all wore a healthy but rather downcast look. Some, in deed, held up their heads and appeared as light hearted as though they were the conquerors, instead of the conquered; but the most of them looked rather sober. They expressed themselves much pleased with Texas, and acknowledged that they had been very kindly treated since they were made prisoners.

One smart looking young fellow remarked that he believed they were better off as prisoners than they were before, because now they had a prospect of getting back home alive; and before it was decidedly problematical! Several negroes were seen among the prisoners; one wearing "bracelets" was an escaped slave. One clothed in sailor's uniform was very much observed, especially among the boys in the crowd, who failed not to improve the occasion for sport.

289

The appearance of the Yankee prisoners marching up Main Street was novel in the extreme, and was a sight which did one good to look at. Although our people were wrought up to the highest pitch of excitement, they conducted themselves with becoming moderation toward the prisoners. Occasionally a boy or two would hoot, but aside from this they were not molested during their whole march.

Altogether they were a fine looking body of men, and ought to be ashamed of themselves for volunteering their services in the villainy of trying to subjugate a chivalrous people.

Discussion

1. Why do you suppose the train was stopped before reaching the station?
2. How did the Yankees feel about their capture?
3. How had they been treated in Texas?
4. What did the boys think of them?

A Hymn of the Confederacy
by O.M.A. (unknown), 1863

*President Jefferson Davis set aside March 27, 1863, as a day
of fasting and prayer for the Confederacy. This hymn, or prayer,
was written by a soldier in camp at Velasco to be used for the
occasion. It was suggested as a Confederate national song.*

While on our guilty land
God lays his chastening hand
   Our sins to scourge;
Father! give us to see
How we have slighted Thee,
And by repentance flee
   From ruin's verge.

O God! we would repent,
And make acknowledgment
   Of errors past;
Pardon for all receive,
To Thee allegiance give,
And in Thy favor live,
   Ever steadfast.

While war's dread havoc reigns,
And rapine stalks our plains,
   Oh, be Thou near!
Our cruel foes restrain,
And drive them back again,
Our country's cause maintain,
   O Saviour, hear!

On Thee our trust is stayed,
Thy power has been displayed
    In our defense.
Still may we claim Thy care,
Thy kind protection share;
Our bleeding country spare,
    Omnipotence!

God of our fathers, hear;
Answer the nation's prayer,
    Which now we make;
From war grant us release,
Bid rage of battle cease,
Oh, give our country peace
    For Jesus' sake!

Some Old Time Advertisements
1863-65

These advertisements appeared in the Houston Tri-Weekly Telegraph.

A Runaway

April 1, 1863.

$100 REWARD—Ran away from E. M. Patrick & Co., of Anderson, Grimes County, boy Tom, about 40 or 45 years of age, carpenter by trade, black complexion, rather inclined to tawny, has no mark that can be remembered except a scar on one of his legs, supposed to be right leg. Tom was purchased from Mr. Grainger, of this place, and by Mr. Grainger from Dr. Shelby of Liberty, where it is supposed Tom is trying to get to. The above reward will be paid on delivery of said negro to J. S. & J. D. Sydnor, Houston, or to E. M. Patrick & Co., Anderson, Grimes County.

High Prices

April 29, 1863.

SALE OF NEGROES—Yesterday the sale of the negroes belonging to Gen. H. P. Bee, took place at the auction rooms of Col. J. S. Sydnor, and the prices ranged beyond those paid a week or two since. The number sold yesterday was 31, and the amount of the sale was between eighty-five and eighty-six thousand dollars. Women from

18 to 20 years of age, sold for $4,000 and $4,500 (Confederate money). One woman with two small children sold for $5,700. Ordinary negro men brought over $4,000. The lot was not an extraordinarily good one, though very fair, but the prices were unusually high.

A Big Auction Sale

January 9, 1865.

J. S. & J. D. Sydnor will sell, without reserve, on Tuesday, January 10th, the first thirty negroes in this advertisement.

1, 2, Violet, dark, 34 years old, and her child Texas, 3 years old, tawny—a cotton picker and field hand and a superior weaver and spinner, washer and ironer. Family long-lived, her grandmother now living at the age of 120 years.

3, 4, Winnie, 18 years old, dark, and her child, one year old, griff.

5, 6, Harriet, 17 years old, and her child, one year old, tawny.

Winnie and Harriet are superior cotton pickers and spinners. The overseer says the two together average their 500 pounds clean cotton per day. They are children of Violet.

7, Fanny, 16 years old, rich black color, field hand exclusively, and remarkably stout.

8, Delia, 14 years old, a bacon skin color, field hand, and very likely; not so stout as other members of her family.

9, Emmeline, 12 years old, dark, very sprightly; can spin her five and six cuts per day; capable of being made a most extraordinary servant.

10, Tom, 10 years old, black; like the balance of the family.

11, Fayette, 8 years old, black; likewise after the same order; as yet has done nothing except to nurse children.

The above embrace one entire family; being of the family that have lived from 75 to 125 years, and have never been out of the family that raised them.

26, Peter, 16 years old, jet black, perfectly trusty, and has never been whipped.

27, Billy, 16 years old, black, rather low in stature, and decidedly handsome, and very intelligent, ingenious and thrifty.

28, Dick, 17 years old, black; as handsome a nigger as can be seen, retiring in his manner—a good field hand.

Titles to all of the above negroes indisputable.

Discussion

1. What means did owners adopt to recover runaway slaves?
2. How old a "boy" was Mr. Patrick's Tom?
3. Were slaves ever taught trades?
4. Make a list of occupations in which the different members of Violet's family were employed.

Raising Money for the War
1863-65

These following appeared in the Houston Tri-Weekly Telegraph.

CONTRIBUTIONS

January 14, 1863.

We acknowledge $20 from Col. L. W. Groce, and $50 from Miss Ellen Groce, for the Rangers' concert.

MR. EDITOR: The teachers and pupils of the Methodist Sabbath School of this city have knit and presented the Confederate army with one hundred and forty pairs of good socks. Who will do likewise?
I. O. CHURCH, Sup't.
Waco

January 26, 1863.

The thanks of the Second regiment Texas volunteers are returned to Mrs. T. J. Hunter, President of the Ladies Aid Society, of Fort Bend County, for 44 pairs woolen socks and 3 woolen neckties. Other contributions for this brave regiment will be thankfully received, and forwarded to them, if left at T. W. House's store.

February 2, 1863.

We received four carpet blankets, two pairs pants, One waistcoat, four pairs socks from Mrs. John A. Campbell, Austin, which we sold to the Clothing Bureau for $83.50. This amount has been deposited in the fund for Sibley's brigade.

CONFEDERATE STATES HOSPITAL,
HEMPSTEAD, Texas,
Nov. 17, 1864.

ED. TELEGRAPH: I desire to return thanks through your widely circulated paper for a donation to this Hospital of one hundred and thirty-three sheep, by Mr. Joe Cavett, of Wheelock, Robertson County, Texas.

Very respectfully, your ob'd't serv't,

E. W. ROGERS,
Assistant Surgeon in Charge.

AMATEUR THEATRICALS

January 23, 1863.

An amateur Dramatic Association is about being formed in this city (Houston) for the purpose of raising funds for the support of soldiers' families. Those who wish to join an affair of this kind can address "Drama," through the post office.

January 23, 1863.

We have received through Capt. C. S. Longcope, four hundred and seventy-three dollars, the proceeds of a concert and tableaux, given by the ladies of La Grange, for the benefit of Dr. L. A. Bryan's Hospital. Of this sum, the following were donations: From Governor Lubbock, $50; A. R. Gates, $50; J. A. Haynie, $50; M. Cavanaugh, $50; G. Markman, $10; Mrs. Sharp, $2; total, $212.

February 2, 1863.

EDITOR TELEGRAPH: The young ladies of Baylor University propose to do something for the benefit of that most deserving corps, the Sibley brigade. They will give an entertainment, consisting of music, tableaux, etc., on Friday night, February 13, which they flatter themselves will prove acceptable to the public.

ANDERSON, GRIMES COUNTY,
January 13, 1863.

EDITOR TELEGRAPH: Herewith find inclosed $100, net proceeds of a concert given, unsolicited, in this place, by three negroes belonging to Capt. D. D. Atcheson. These negroes formerly lived in Galveston, and say they wish the money expended for the benefit of those wounded in defense of their late city home. Acknowledge receipt and turn over to proper person or persons.

Respectfully,
M.

January 19, 1863.

The three negroes belonging to Captain Atcheson, who gave a concert and thus raised $100 for the benefit of the wounded in the Galveston fight, are worthy of honorable mention. They have done a good thing and should have credit for it.

A FANCY DRESS PARTY

January 23, 1863.

On Friday evening a social party and an elegant supper will be given by the ladies of Houston and Galveston, the proceeds of which are to be given to the sick, wounded, and indigent soldiers in and about the two cities. The arrangements for the supper are on a scale of elegance unsurpassed heretofore, and we can promise those who go a good time. Tickets of admission will be for sale at the usual places on the street. Those who may not be able, or do not wish to attend, are requested to send their contributions in money to the editor of this paper.

Flag Song of Texas
by Lee C. (Leah Cohen) Harby

O prairie breeze, blow sweet and pure,
And Southern sun shine bright
To bless our flag, where'er may gleam
Its single star of light;
But should the sky grow dark with wrath,
The tempest burst and rave,
It still shall float undauntedly,
The standard of the brave!

(Chorus)
Flag of our State, O glorious flag!
Unsullied in peace, and triumphant in war;
Heroes have fought for you,
Statesmen have wrought for you—
Emblazoned in glory you bear the Lone Star!

By deeds of arms our land was freed,
And priceless the reward!
Brave Milam died and Fannin fell
Its sacred rights to guard;
Our patriot force with mighty will
Triumphant set it free,
And Travis, Bowie, Crockett gave
Their lives for liberty!

And when on San Jacinto's plain
The Texians heard the cry,
"Remember, men, the Alamo!"
They swore to win or die;
Resistless in their high resolve,
They forced the foe to yield,
And freedom crowned their victory
On that illustrious field!

O Texas, tell the story o'er,
With pride recall each name,
And teach your sons to emulate
Their virtues and their fame;
So shall your grandeur still increase,
Your glory shine afar,
For deathless honor guards the flag
Where gleams the proud Lone Star!

In 1902 Hon. William L. Prather, L.L. D., President of The University of Texas, placed at the disposal of the Daughters of the Republic of Texas $100 to be offered as a prize for the best song on the subject of the Texas Flag. They conducted a contest and awarded the prize to Mrs. Harby for this poem.